AF365851

NATHANIEL

REIKI
the path
of three
DIAMONDS

The Path to
Spiritual Harmony

A deeper
understanding of
Reiki through the
integration of three
spiritual forces

Indie publishing, 2015

A State of Mind

http://astateofmind.eu

Additional Credit:
Cover Photo: Daibutsu from Kamakura, Japan. Photo by Andrea Schaffer, source: Flickr <https://www.flickr.com/photos/aschaf/3801559699> (Creative Commons BY 2.0). Font used: OptimusPrinceps, by Manfred Klein.

Table of Contents

There are Three Diamonds:
Of Earth, Heaven and Heart
When the Diamonds become One
The Man becomes One.
Reiki is the path of Earth.
It teaches us about our Great Mother.
She offers Life, food and shelter.
Reiki is the path of Heaven.
It teaches us about our Great Father.
He offers hope, love and strength.
Reiki is the path of Heart.
With it, we can see ourselves
In the eyes of all living beings.

Notes for Good Start

Remember – you can become a Reiki practitioner only through proper attunement (initiation), that is passed onto you by a Reiki teacher as you attend the first degree (Shoden) workshop/class. While you can learn how to practice Reiki from books, articles or recordings, the ability to work with Reiki itself must be passed through attunement process.

***

This book presents my personal perspective upon Reiki practice.

It is not „the only traditional approach", nor the definitely correct approach. Nevertheless, I hope that some of you will find this work inspiring and you will benefit from reading it.

Reiki: A Path of Self-Growth through Spiritual Self-Healing

In the Western world, Reiki is considered mainly a form of complementary therapy that is used to support classic forms of therapies. Thus, Reiki is used at home, at medical facilities, hospitals, animal care facilities and at other places, where it brings positive benefits. But as far as we understand it today, „Reiki as therapy" was not the intend of the method's creator, Mikao Usui, when he created his system of healing. We believe that Usui have created the path of Reiki as a path of personal self-healing practice, and this self-healing was meant to help in spiritual growth progress. The *Tenohira*[1], that is healing by laying on of hands, was

---

1   *Tenohira* relates to healing by placing the hands on the body in a specific way, for example, through particular hand positions. In case of Reiki, we can

merely a part of the more complex system of traditional practice.

This book is meant to present you the method of Reiki as a path of inner growth. It is meant to help you understand why do we use some of the techniques in Reiki, what is their deeper meaning and why some experiences are common for every practitioner on this Reiki path. But before we do so, some terms and ideas must be explained and mentioned, as we cannot practice without some basic understanding.

Thus, let's begin with defining what Reiki is. This definition will serve this book perfectly.[2] Books and articles provide us with multiple definitions. For the purpose of this book, we will slightly ignore (to some degree) the idea that Reiki is just energy. We won't consider Reiki just a method of working with energy, either. Both of those are interesting definitions, good for manuals and books and Reiki classes, but for the purpose of this book, we will use a different definition.

We shall understand Reiki as a term pointing us to a specific school of thought – the Usui Shiki Ryoho Reiki. According to this school, trying to create the proper definition, we shall say that: **Reiki is a practice, that once applied on regular basis in our daily life, brings us back to the state of harmony, both the inner harmony with ourselves, and the outer harmony with our environment. The practice of Reiki brings back the state of Unity.**

In those few words, Reiki becomes no longer just energy and just a method of working with energy. It becomes a practice, and the

---

encounter another word, *teate,* that refers to healing through touch, but in a non-standard way.

2   These days I believe there are three definitions of Reiki. The first definition explains Reiki for the purpose of Western therapy. The second definition explains Reiki as a traditional spiritual practice. And the third definition is the personal definition that every Reiki practitioner makes for himself/herself.

practice becomes a part of our daily life. This practice is made of five fundamental elements, that will be explained in this book. In addition, what's interesting and very useful, is that Reiki itself does not become the only life path or spiritual path, if the practitioner does not wish so. The five elements of Reiki practice can be successfully implemented as a part of some other spiritual practice of inner-growth. Reiki, that said, is a complementary, and universal practice.

And definitely, Reiki is a path of learning – on this path, we learn in many ways. We learn from books that we read, from texts that we study, and from lectures that we listen to. The Buddhists believe that even listening to a teacher or studying sacred texts and knowledge is already a huge step on the path to our personal enlightenment. In addition, we learn from our own life experiences.

Knowledge is gained from books, workshops, lectures, while wisdom is gained by experiencing life, and learning from every single experience that life offers us. And the life offers us lessons all the time. But in order for the knowledge and wisdom to develop, often we need to get rid of the useless things we carry in our mind and heart first. This reminds me of an old and well-known tale about a monk and a teacher.

> An old, well-respected teacher went to a Buddhist monk for further teachings, so that he could improve his knowledge. The monk sat down, and the teacher begun to ask questions. He kept asking and there was no end to the stream of his words. Suddenly, the monk begun to pour the tea into a cup. He kept doing so, until the tea begun to spill out from the cup, and even so the monk didn't stop pouring the tea in.

- What are you doing?! - screamed the teacher.

The monk put the kettle aside, looked at the teacher and said.

- Like this cup, so is your mind. How can I teach you anything new if your mind is already full?

The teacher understood what the monk meant. In order to gain new knowledge, we must empty our mind first. [3]

Like in the tale posted above, you, too, must forget about many things that you have learned in the past. Especially if you've been limited by a belief that Reiki is merely a form of energetic therapy or alternative healing method, because it's a way more than just that.

A person that practice Reiki on regular basis in his or hers heart, mind and soul, by taking care of the five fundamental elements: the self-treatment, meditations, five precepts, four mantras and symbols and the blessing of Reiju (the attunement)[4], this is the person that will rediscover what Reiki truly is, as the three diamonds will be integrated into wholeness. Those three diamonds are the metaphorical elements/energies/forces of earth, heaven and heart. According to the general teachings of China and Japan, these energies make all that exists. And Reiki is the path of uniting the three diamonds. This book is exactly about this process of unification and integration of the mentioned three precious,

---

3   This story is interesting in the context of our daily life. Often, we ask for new experiences or material goods, but they won't come. And how should they come if there is no more room for them in our life? Sometimes, we need to get rid of the old stuff in order to make room for new stuff.

4   The western attunement is not the same thing as traditional Reiju – but to simplify things, I will use both these terms in this book, because the result of the attunement and the Reiju is still the very same. More details on this will be explained in dedicated chapter of this book.

spiritual forces.

Searching for the Answers Within Yourself

As Frans Stiene said, the outer Reiki teacher is only here to help you find the inner teacher within you. That said, to continue from my own perspective, in reality there is only one teacher – Reiki. And only one student – you. This is a „reiki-specific" thought that translates as a universal truth: there is only one teacher: the highest spiritual power some people call The Universe, God, Absolute, the Great Spirit. You are the only student – this truth remains unchanged.

A lot of people seeks life guideposts and tips for good living in spiritual techniques and paths. They seek a better life. Religions and ideologies provide the believers with sacred books and thoughts of great philosophers. Things like this are nowhere to be found in the practice of Reiki. In this method, the only guidelines are called „Reiki Precepts", traditionally known as Gokai. Some people like to acknowledge the Waka poems as an additional guide into spirituality. The Gokai are universal and are unrelated to any specific religion or ideology. The Waka are the effect of work of a Japanese emperor Meiji, who ruled Japan at the lifespan of Usui Mikao. The organization somehow created by Usui, the Usui Reiki Ryoho Gakkai, tells us that Usui associated the Waka poems to the practice of Reiki in order to provide the students with additional ethical guidelines.

But other sources tells us that Usui added the Waka poems to his teachings only because of the state politics. It is said that at the era of Meiji, anything that was anti-government was not welcomed in Japan – acting against the Emperor could lead people to jail. Even spiritual groups such as the one lead by Usui were suspicious in the eyes of the government. The government tried to make sure such groups would not oppose the state religion of Shinto. In order to provide political safety to his teachings, Usui is said to strongly advice studies of Waka poems to his students.[5] Today, we are unsure if Usui have seen a spiritual benefit in Waka poems, or was it just a political step. Still, it doesn't matter that much – because even today we can acknowledge the fact that the Meiji's Waka poems can provide a great anchor for contemplation on ethics and spirituality – even if it is not considered to be an integral part of Reiki system by most.

Let's go back to the main subject. Is there anything but Gokai and Waka in the practice of Reiki that may act as an ethical guide to proper living? While it's agreeable that Reiki has some of its roots in the paths of Shinto, Taoism and Buddhism, none of this paths is directly, strongly related to the Usui Shiki Ryoho Reiki. This is where we reach the final reality: the practice of Reiki leads us to realize that we, as Reiki practitioners and as individuals, should stop searching for knowledge int he outside world, and begin to seek knowledge within ourselves. Each one of us carries all the answers we need in ourselves. It's a path of our nature, whether we call it the state of primal humanity, or the Nature of Buddha. The practice of Reiki does not tells us „do not read and do not listen" - this is useful, but it's only a part of the idea. In reality, the practice tells us simple things: practice Reiki, contemplate upon the Gokai, and that which is really important for your life will come to you when you're ready to accept it.

That is why this book shows you only the techniques, the information about the (potential) roots of Reiki practice, historical knowledge and it provides you with some basic understanding of general spiritual growth. This book tries not to provide you with

---

5   Petter, F. A., *This is Reiki.*

ethical tips and stuff. You can seek specific inspirations or wise quotes in other sources, or by living among people. Reiki can show you only that which is already within you – and there are great inspirations, life tips and suggestions there, as well as the reasons why your life is unsuccessful – once these reasons are recognized and healed, your life shall change for better.

Understanding Reiki

A person who wish to discover what Reiki really is, must integrate two archetypes within himself or herself. The first archetype is the image of an European student of secret teaching, who sits among books, notes, covered by a dim light of candles, who takes great effort in understanding the sense of things. A Reiki practitioner must be like this student of secrets: study books, tomes, articles, notes and expand his or hers knowledge in any way possible. A person that stops gaining knowledge may never become a Reiki master. But this is just the beginning – because at some point, a different archetype must take the place of the first one.

This second archetype is the image of an Eastern wise man who meditates and seeks answers through various esoteric practices,[6] which means inner practices – he seeks answers in his inner self, and not in the books. By the inner practice of Reiki, the practitioner is capable of integrating the forces of earth and heaven in his or hers own heart, thus opening the doors leading to enlightenment. Only through personal experience the practitioner can understand the knowledge gained from books.

The work you're reading right now is one of the many steps that lead to integrating the first archetype into your own life. This book is meant to provide you with knowledge and direct you further to

---

6   Greek *esôterikos* – inner, on the inside.

more advanced sources of knowledge. But only if you take this book to a practical level, through personal experience and realization of the second archetype, you can fully understand the wisdom of that which became a part of your Reiki experience. Thus, do not forget to practice Reiki, because in reality you are the only person that can heal your own life.

***

So far for the introduction. Let's move to a more important aspect of defining that which we call „healing" and „spiritual growth". In addition, I will explain some common elements of spiritual practice, that may become a part of your life once you begin to work with Reiki.

Self-Healing and Personal Growth - Defined

We should define the terms of self-healing and personal growth in the context of practicing Reiki. Basically, this process of definition is going to be explored through the next couple of chapters, because we must discuss a bit of history, but also a bit of ideas and concepts that often become a part of Reiki practitioner's life and experience. Only then we can understand many aspects of the Reiki practice itself.

In the entire process of self-healing and healing in general we do not talk about the idea of Western medicine, but about the healing as the process of bringing harmony back with yourself and harmony with the outside world. The practice of Reiki is not focused on healing diseases, but on brining unity back with ourselves that with everything that surrounds us. The regression of the illness becomes merely a side effect of such spiritual healing. Because we talk about healing in the primal and essential meaning of this word. The shamans and healers of multiple traditions agree on the basic idea of what healing is about. A healer and writer, Galsan Tschinag, said:

> Healing is the process of bringing order to the way we think, to the way we perceive the world.[7]

Based on the knowledge of healers from all around the world, Geseko von Lupke says:

> According to shamans and healers, the illness is the disharmony of forces that exist in the person and in the cosmos. In healthy people, these forces work and act together in a correct way. We become ill when these life forces cannot flow through us undisrupted.
>
> This disharmony makes negative and disharmonious energies settle in our body and spirit. The energies take control and become visible as the symptoms of the illness.
>
> The task of the healer is all about getting rid of those negative energies, get rid of the energetic blockages and bring harmony back to the physical body. (...) The shamans (...) approach this energy, this state, this spirit, with great compassion.
>
> (...)
>
> It is passed onto the ill person that he or she is responsible for the loss of the harmony in his or hers body. Thus, he or she is solely responsible for bringing harmony back. Once the person begins to live in agreement with his

---

7   Lupke, G. von, *Dawna mądrość na nowe czasy*, p. 114.

or hers goals, hopes and needs – the person regains health. If these needs, hopes and goals are not lived by, the person gets ill. This definition is similar to the definition made by the World Health Organization, according to which health is a state of complete physical, psychological and social well-being of a person, and it's not merely a lack of illness.[8]

Later on, we read:

> Shamanic healing is about renewing the contact – on both the inner and outer level – with the Nature and the soul. (...) [Shamans] „make visible the things that were invisible. The process of healing is about brining to light the things that were covered by darkness.[9]

Of course, the Reiki practitioner is not a shaman. He do not perceive, like shamans and healers often do, the illness as a result of acts made by malicious spirits. Still, perhaps because of the archetypal understanding, even the Reiki practitioner recognize illness, both the physical and mental one, as a disruption in the inner and outer harmony. Healing is the process of creating harmony between the elements of the microcosm and macrocosm. From the perspective of Reiki, what we see is the process of integration of the Three Diamonds: of the Earth, Heaven and Heart. It is this process that occurs in Reiki practitioner as a result of personal practice. It also occurs in the person that benefits from regular Reiki treatments, although in a lower scale.

This integration, thus the return of harmony, is visible on many

---

8   Ibidem, p. 35-37

9   Ibidem, p. 40

levels, starting with smaller things like creating harmony in our diet or work, through the psychological elements like the integration of the unconscious mind, that is healing of emotions and memories (the Jungian Shadow), up to the higher aspects of spirituality, finding our own individual spiritual path or even our final destiny.

Mikao Usui created the method of Reiki, so that this method can help every person rediscover what a human being actually is. Self-healing in case of Reiki, that is a process of personal growth, is a process of rediscovering our true nature – let's call it the state of primal humanity, or the Buddha's Nature. This harmonious Buddha's Nature is a part of every person. The purpose of spiritual practices is to help every individual person rediscover this nature and integrate it into this person's daily life, on the physical, emotional/mental and spiritual level. In the practice of Reiki, the Three Diamonds are symbolically showed in the Kanji Reiki – the symbol of the method – through the tree squares in the *Rei* symbol. Traditionally, these squares represent hungry mouths of people. In the context of Reiki, it's the spiritual food that we're talking about, a food for those three levels – the spiritual, emotional/mental and physical. That's what I'm referring to in this book, the three diamonds: of Earth (physical), Heaven (emotional/mental) and Heart (spiritual)

In the context of the Reiki practice, self-healing is a process of brining serenity and unity with ourselves and our environment through the use of multiple techniques. The disappearance of physical illness is merely a side effect of healing of our unconscious mind and human soul. A person that heals his soul, will experience, physical health, abundance and prosperity, as well as happiness that comes with self-realization.

Now that we understand what healing is (in short) and how we can define personal growth (that's the process of self-healing), we can move on and see what are the roots of Reiki method.

East and West – The Insights

To understand the practice of Reiki better, you can familiarize yourself with geographical and cultural roots of the discussed method. It's obvious that the method itself originates from Japan. The entire Far East is covered by a mysterious mist and romantic mystery, as presented in the Western society. Neither the globalization neither the fact that a lot of our gadgets has been made there, helps us dispel this mist.

Japan is dominated by an animistic religion of Shinto. It's a country, in which everything that exists is considered to be sacred – at least this is the perspective of the elders, before the „civilized" West came to Japan. We may distinguish two elements of the fall of Shinto in Japan – first when the era of Meiji emperor came to be, and then after the II World War, when the economical boom became more important that the environment or the culture of Japan. After the II World War, the importance of Shinto faded away due to the reforms made by the allied occupational forces. Today, the reborn of some „sacred land" ideas can be seen in the growing ecological movement or food cooperatives.[10] Although we won't experience the Japan as Mikao Usui experienced it during his life those 100 years ago, the memory of the old Japan is alive.

Japan is a country of complex etiquette, one which would be considered too complex and too rigid according to Western standards. It's also a country heavily influenced by Buddhism.

The culture of the Far East can be characterized with many things – one of these things, that is very important to us, is the

---

10 Hall, J.W., *Japonia od czasów najdawniejszych do dzisiaj*, p. 290.

tendency for introspection, so popular in Japan. This tendency, slowly pushed away by the Western culture, is the very first thing that makes us wonder deeply about the nature of the system of Reiki.

D.T. Suzuki, in one of his lectures, makes a clear distinction between the members of the Western and Eastern cultures. The members of the Western cultures can be characterized with more logical, scientific approach to life, and with an analytical mind, that must rethink everything from an intellectual perspective. Rationality, logic and intellect, those are the things that govern the mind of the Western man, who constantly experience a state of separation from the Nature. The man of the West is not a part of nature in his own eyes – he is the lord and researcher of the Nature, ready to spread destruction in order to make a vivisection and learn the ways the World operates. Compared to this, the man of the East is an integral part of Nature – he feels as a part of Nature. He rarely analyze the World around him and is not a subject to chaotic influence of the intellect. He observes, he „**is**", he experiences things through intuition, and directs his focus towards inner self. He does not destroys the Nature, but contemplates it.[11] He seeks answers to great questions within himself, and not in the outside realm. Reiki is best perceived through this Eastern perspective – through the states of intuition, directing focus towards the inner self, and the feeling of connection to the entire World. Reiki suggests that the answers to the outer questions can be found in the inner world of our heart and mind. In the practice of Reiki, due to the nature of this method and the Reiki energy, we must place the Western rationality aside – and we must trust our own heart and intuition.

---

11 De Martino, R., Fromm, E., Suzuki, D. T., *Buddyzm zen i psychoanaliza*, p. 11-21.

Years ago, I used to observe discussions about the modern spiritual paths of the man of the West. The problem often pointed out by the Elders was too blind approach to spirituality as presented by the New Age movement. In this approach, everyone can take anything from any spiritual path, anything that fits this person's point of view – without thinking about his or hers choice. The wise Elders said that it may be difficult to understand the specific spiritual path if we won't study its roots and complexity, or the cultural context of this spiritual path.

It took me many years to understand that there was great wisdom in the words of Elders. By walking the path of Reiki, one day I understood that the Elders were right – it's very important to understand the cultural context of the spiritual practice in order to understand it better, especially if we wish to make this practice a part of our daily life. In case of this book, in order to really understand Reiki and benefit from this practice, we must understand a few things: the cultural context of Buddhism, Taoism and Shinto, as well as the culture of Japan, even in its short form.

In the old Japan, a man was characterized by introspection – constant readiness and willingness to look into his own heart and mind. This element of Japanese culture was present for many hundreds of years, and it's one of the elements of the cultural context of Reiki, that cannot be forgotten. This context tells us one thing – if we want to benefit greatly from the practice of Reiki, we must turn out attention to our own inner self. Can we do anything else if we're practicing something that originates from such introvert culture?

Somebody may wish to run towards non-esoteric practice and use Reiki in form of treatments on others, considering Reiki as a form of therapy. This is a great way to use Reiki and it's worthy to continue this path, but one of the unwritten rules of Reiki says:

first, heal yourself. On the path of Reiki, the esoteric practice is the most important aspect. The word „esoteric" originates from Greek „esôterikos" that can be translated as „focused inward". In Reiki, focus on your inner self, the process of introspection, is the most important thing – this is the practice of self-healing.

And this is the practice of inner growth.

Reiki as a Path of Inner Growth

Reiki is not a religion – but it can become an individual life ideology, as well as individual spiritual path. While religion can be characterized with heaving a priest class, central deity (or deities), and a dogmatic collection of practices, the spiritual path on the other hand is based solely on personal experiences, that may or may not confirm the theoretical knowledge provided by books.

Some sources say that Mikao Usui wished to create an universal method of healing and inner growth,[12] while other sources say that Usui went to Mount Kurama with sole purpose of preparing himself for death and reborn in the Buddhist paradise.[13] Finally, more eclectic sources merge these two theories together and say that Usui went to Mount Kurama with a purpose of experiencing the whole of human experience and discovering his own Buddha's Nature. In case he would not be successful, he was prepared to die – this was his final goal on a long path of spiritual practice and studies – become enlighten or die.

In result, thanks to his practices and mystical satori, Mikao Usui achieved his goal, developed an universal method of self-healing and spiritual growth – this method turned out to be directly disconnected to all other religions or ideologies. That said, Mikao

---

12 Stiene, B., Stiene F., *Japanese Art of Reiki*, p. 7.

13 Petter, F. A., *This is Reiki.*

Usui was a Buddhist and while creating the system of Reiki, he kept the Buddhist ideals in his mind – the ideals of compassion for all living beings, an ideal popular in the path of Mahayana Buddhism and its Bodhisattva concept. Frans Petter writes:

> Practicing Reiki Ryoho means to wish happiness, health and wellbeing to all beings.[14]

When, due to Reiki practice, you will awake the great compassion for all living beings, you understand the true power of Reiki. Compassion in the concept of Buddhism is one of the cultural ideas that are our companion on the path of Usui Shiki Ryoho Reiki.

The Falls on the Path of Self-Healing

Before I proceed with Compassion, I wish to discuss one of the primary concepts in Buddhism, that have a great meaning for a Reiki practitioner. I remind you that, like so often in Reiki, this concept is, in its essence, neutral and universal. This concept refers to a process of spiritual growth. It was nicely explained by Sangharakszita in his book, „What is Dharma?"[15]

This process goes like this: first, we define the intention of growth and development (self-healing), and then we begin the practice, for example: meditation. Through meditation, we can reach many wonderful mental and spiritual states of mind, in which we can remain for minutes, hours or even weeks. But then, we experience a sudden fall – we go back to what our life looked like before spiritual growth – we go back to things that kicked us out from the state of harmony. This process of falling on the path

---

14 Ibidem, p. 50.

15 Sangharakszita, *Czym jest Dharma? Podstawy nauki Buddy,* p. 141-147.

of spiritual growth is quite normal, because the spiritual practice, whatever it is, is merely a tool that helps us reach a certain point.

Thus, do not be surprised if, after many months, or even years of practicing Reiki, suddenly you fall down – and the things, which you wished to heal, suddenly return. Do not blame yourself and do not think that you're someone worse than others, because you „do not get the results others get". Perhaps those „others" do not talk loudly about their falls and mistakes?

The path of spiritual growth is a path of constant rise and fall. Be aware of this fact and do not get disappointed. Remember that the true strength of a human being is not the fact that the man never falls – the strength is in our ability to get up from every fall. Each time you fall on the path of spirituality, get up! Go back to practicing, if you have experienced results in the past. If you see the results, then keep practicing and do not worry if you fail from time to time – this is especially important for the practitioners of the second and third Reiki degree, Okuden and Shinpiden respectfully.

Such constant falling on the spiritual path and returns of things we thought were already healed, all of this has a meaning. The meaning is to show us that we haven't healed something entirely. Each time a problem returns is an opportunity to heal a bit more of it, understand and experience it a bit more, once again. If we've been healing the problem long enough, through multiple returns of the problem, this problem gets healed entire at last – the results become permanent, as our understanding and awareness of things become clear.

Of course, we do not wish for our path of self-healing to lead to constant failures. The Buddhist teachings explain that failures come to an end when, thanks to spiritual practice, we develop our inner Wisdom. Wisdom, as understood by Buddhism, is a constant

„awareness of reality and of Unconditioned."[16] It's about looking through the veil and noticing the real causes or events and experiences. In Reiki practice, we manifest this state of awareness step by step, slowly and gently. By understanding the mechanisms that condition our experiences, we begin to accept both the experiences and the mechanisms. Furthermore, we accept our inner Shadow, which I will discuss later in this book. Also, we develop our individual wisdom and the ability to see the mechanisms leading to life events. This is a path towards a place, in which we no longer fall on the path of spirituality.

If you practice Reiki long enough, with pure intentions and open heart, then you will develop your inner wisdom. This wisdom will protect you against falling on the path of self-healing, and this healing state will be experienced by you more often and for longer periods of time in more and more aspects of your life.

Reiki is a Mean Leading to a Goal

Reiki is a practice that leads to harmony, health and happiness, and maybe even to the final enlightenment. I emphasize the word „path", because Reiki is not the goal in itself. When you work with Reiki only for the purpose of working with Reiki, the practice of this method leads you nowhere. Just like this, the Buddhist Dharma is not a goal in itself, but it's a path that leads to the final goal – enlightenment. When you study the Buddhism, you may encounter a story of a raft. The raft is meant to cross water. It's the ultimate and only purpose of the raft. The Dharma is like a raft. Some people begin to build walls on the raft, add furniture, decorate it. Other people worship the raft, but never use it to cross the water. Even more people criticize that the raft is not strong

---

16 Ibidem

enough.[17] Very similar approach can be noticed on the path of Reiki. Reiki is, too, like a raft – it's a mean that helps us achieve a goal, but Reiki is not a goal by itself. There's also a Japanese tale of a finger pointing to the moon – it's not the finger that's important here. It only points the goal – once the glow of the moon is noticed, it becomes far more important that the finger itself.

Do not focus on the „Reiki raft" too much – use this method to achieve happiness if you wish it. And remember that Buddha used to say that we should practice only things that bring us real, positive results. If something gives you no results, then there's no reason to practice it. In the Kalama Sutra we generally read:

> Have trust in things, which you learned to be true after long search; have trust in things, that you know they bring wellbeing to you and to others.[18]

Your belief in the practice should be based only upon your own experience, and not on the words of other practitioners or teachers. If Reiki gives you positive results, then keep practicing. If Reiki gives you no positive results even if you've been practicing intensively for a long time, then perhaps it's time to give up this path. Even if every person can learn Reiki, this method won't be suitable for everyone. It's because every person is different and unique. Some people will prefer Reiki, other people will prefer Buddhist path, and others will prefer psychotherapy or a personal development coach. Don't stick forcefully to something that gives you no results.

One more tip for your personal growth. Remember that Reiki will guide you in accordance with your own nature. There are not

---

17 Ibidem

18 http://www.accesstoinsight.org/lib/authors/soma/wheel008.html

two practitioners that are exactly alike. We're all different. Each Reiki practitioner feels the energy differently, experience the results of Reiki differently and the process of healing and growth of this person is unique. Buddha said that when rain falls upon a seed of a palm, a palm shall grow. If a rain falls on the seed of a flower, a flower will grow. But a flower will never become a palm, and the palm will never become a flower.[19] Each Reiki practitioner will grow according to his or hers own nature.

Every Reiki practitioner will heal things with his own unique means. Every person will practice differently, and every person will understand Reiki differently. Even more, every person will have a unique pace of self-healing. Do not try to resemble other practitioners. Discover yourself and let Reiki lead you on your own, individual path, in accordance to your own needs – this will give you the best results. This is the only way in which Reiki will lead you to the state of harmony, unity and happiness.

Spiritual Growth and its Biggest Enemy – the Ego

Let's now discuss a very important problem that may trouble you on your path of self-healing. I used to say that ego is needed for every person, but only for a time. Before the time to get rid of our ego comes, this ego helps us defend ourselves against manipulation and treachery from the outside world, because it makes us question that, which we find on the path of our own inner growth. Just like everything else, the ego, too, has its light and dark side. The good side is the one that ask questions and makes us wonder and think, question everything that we're about to step into. The bad side is the one that tries to protect itself. Yes, ego tries to protect its very own existence, because it knows, that at some point of spiritual growth, it becomes needless for the person and must

---

19 Sangharakszita, *Czym jest Dharma? Podstawy nauki Buddy*, p. 44-45.

disappear for good.

And ego (its dark side) can find awful ways to trouble us on our path – it can manipulate us in such ways that we won't even notice that we have wondered away from the path of true inner growth – this often happens to people who fall into a trap of New Age movement.

A Buddhist teacher, Sogyal Rinpoche, wrote this about the nature of our ego:

> The reason to end the absolute tyranny of the ego is the reason that we enter the path of spiritual growth.
>
> (…)
>
> At first, as we first become fascinated by the spiritual path and the possibilities it offers us, that it present to us, our ego may try to encourage us, whispering: „This is wonderful, beautiful. At last, it's something for you! These teachings are great!"
>
> (…)
>
> But as soon as we enter [specific time] of spiritual growth and the teachings we study will finally reveal their deep meaning to us, inevitably we face the truth about ourselves. When the ego is truly revealed and sensitive areas of ourselves become apparent, problems are obvious to follow. It's like a mirror appears in front of us and we can't turn our eyes away. (…) We begin to fight it [the truth about ourselves] because we hate that which we see in this mirror.
>
> (…) And where's the ego? It stands faithfully on our side and whispers: „You're right, this is outrageous and unbearable. Give up this whole spiritual growth thing."
>
> (…)

The ego is happy to see as we fall into its own trap. For the pain, loneliness and problems we face, it cast blame upon the teachings and the teachers. The final weapon of the ego is to point the finger on the teacher and his students, whispering: „I don't think so anyone here lives by the teachings!"[20]

This process is not easy. First, we are being encouraged to walk the path of spiritual growth. In the context of Reiki, the teachers promise us health, harmony, happiness, love, wonderful business, inner peace and things like that. At first, everything is wonderful, but then – doubt comes into play. Because at some point, we begin to see the truth about ourselves, and this truth is often unpleasant and we don't like it. But know that what happens here is merely the beginning of the awareness of our inner Shadow. Here we stand on the crossroads – we can either accept the truth about ourselves and self-heal ourselves; or we can deny this truth, give up the Reiki practice and our own inner growth.

But if you do continue the [spiritual growth] practice and you enter deeper states of meditation, slowly you realize that you became a victim of the ego's promises: false hopes and false fears.[21]

Christian mysticism in the European culture calls such crisis, as explained above – the doubt that appears – by the name of „dark night of the soul". This experience is similar to the falls on the path of spiritual growth, too. From time to time, such repetitive spiritual crisis may appear in your life, during which you will doubt your

---

20 Rinpocze, S., *Tybetańska Księga Życia i Umierania*, p. 115-116.

21 Ibidem

own spiritual progress, the value of the practice itself, or the point of spiritual teachings. At the same time, from the depths of your unconsciousness, fears and negative thoughts and bad memories or beliefs may emerge. Such crisis may last for days, weeks, months or even years.

When this happens, the best thing to do is to take a break from spiritual matters, do yourself spiritual vacations, and then return to your practice with new motivation and fresh positive approach, and this will give you results – the falls, and crisis will appear less often, and you will notice more and more positive effects of the practice in your daily life.

It's worth to mention how does the spiritual path looks like, according to Buddhist teachings. I mention this because a similar mechanisms can be seen in other schools of spiritual thought. It's all about understanding that ups and downs on the path of spiritual development are quite normal and that they are a tool that polish a diamond of our soul. Recognizing the ups and downs makes us strengthen ourselves in our practice, so that in result we won't lose hope because of the downs that are part of everyone's experience.

At some point of spiritual growth, we pass over a critical point – a point below which we will never fall again. And even if the worse moments will still appear, we will continue to walk forward and grow further. Remember that even on the path of Reiki, the „dark night of the soul" may appear a few times, but after some time, even this experience will be gone for good.

Unfortunately, sometimes it may happen that a person tries to deny the truth about himself or herself and gives up the spiritual teachings or the Reiki practice (as a path), but won't deny the simple aspect of doing Reiki treatments. This is the time when Reiki becomes merely a commercial practice, meant for initiating others, offering workshops and doing treatments – all for money.

But behind such business offer we see no pure heart or honest intentions – those can be developed only through regular and honest spiritual practice. If you feel like you're falling into a trap of „business spirituality", then do a step backwards and look closely upon your own intentions.

Also, be careful with your own ego and watch it closely, as it may set traps on your path, just as Sogyal Rinpoche explained.

Reiki is an Individual Practice

Buddha said:

> Trust the advices of the teacher, and not on the teacher's personality.
> Trust the meanings of teachings, and not on the mere words.
> Trust the deeper meaning, and not the outside meaning.
> Trust the wise mind, and not the ordinary, judging mind.[22]

In this quote, we can find words of wisdom for a Reiki practitioner. Trust the knowledge that is shared with you by the Reiki teacher, instead of relying on the teacher's personality, that never defines the practice itself. Each teacher is different and you should not perceive Reiki through this teacher's lifestyle. Your own personality is different. Rely on the meaning of Reiki knowledge, and not on the words that are used to share this knowledge. Different sources use different words, names and terms, but a sensible Reiki practitioner will be determined to reach the deeper and real meaning that is hidden behind the mere terms and words. Explore the knowledge that you're beginning to comprehend, in order to comprehend it even more. That which seems clear at first,

---

22 Ibidem

often turns out to have a second, much deeper meaning – it's normal for the Reiki practice.

It's worth to mention a bit about modern New Age spirituality that often is encountered by Reiki practitioners. If you wish, Reiki can become your sole spiritual path and as such, it will be beneficial enough for you. That said, don't try to jump from one practice to another, at least don't do so too soon. If you've chosen Reiki as your practical path, then walk this path. If this method seems not beneficial to you at the moment, it may mean that you're experiencing a normal spiritual crisis and you simply need to find more strength.

Sogyal Rinpoche says about similar experiences:

> (…) Do not walk into a trap of something that I observe all the time in the Western world. I call it a „mall mentality” - when people jump from one teacher to another, from one teachings to other teachings, with no continuity or real, serious devotion to a specific practice. Nearly all great masters of spiritual traditions agree to the fact that the best to do is to master a single path, a single road leading to truth, and following with you all your heart and mind a single spiritual tradition till the very end of your spiritual journey, while remaining open and respectful for the wisdom of others. In Tibet, we used to say: „by knowing one, you know them all”. A popular perspective these days that says that we can remain open multiple doors and we should not devote ourselves to anything entirely, is one of the greatest illusions of our time – it's a trick of our ego, one of the strongest tricks that our ego throws at us so that it can hinder our spiritual progress.
>
> If you're still looking for something, looking becomes an

obsession that turns you into a tourist left out of breath, a tourist that never reaches any goal at all.[23]

Sogyal Rinpoche continues to explain that it's not about closing yourself in a cage and limiting your insights into the spiritual world. Quite the opposite. The advice comes from a pure compassion and it's meant to make you remain focused on a single path, so that no matter what the world throws at you, you will not give up the path.

„No matter what" doesn't mean, of course, that you have to keep walking the Reiki path at all costs. The positive results of Reiki can bee seen right away after a few weeks of practice – and definitely after a few months of practice. If you're honest with yourself and you truly wish to heal your life and make it better, then the results will become reality. But if there are no results, eve if you've been practicing honestly and on regular basis, then it may mean that Reiki is not a method meant for you, or that you have no honest intentions for yourself. You need to ask yourself – do you truly wish to be healed?

And what if you will have doubts regarding your own experiences and positive results of Reiki? First, keep in mind that doubts are good, because they make you question your intentions, actions and effectiveness of the practice all the time. But more than that, doubts are normal on every single path of spiritual growth. „Unless we become enlightened, doubts will be experienced surely, because creating chaos and doubt is what an unenlightened mind usually do. The only way to deal with doubts is to try not to embrace the doubt or to suppress it."[24] Thus, do not suppress the doubts, and do not embrace the doubt, just let it go. Sogyal

---

23 Ibidem

24 Ibidem

Rinpoche says that doubts won't go away right away and they won't go away just by themselves. They will go away with time, as a result of regular practice. To have doubts on the path of Reiki is normal. We may even say that having doubts is a privilege of an unenlightened mind.

Do not be afraid of doubts. Let each and every single doubt become an opportunity to contemplate upon your own life, your intentions, dreams, goals and perception of reality.

Teachers, Masters and Lineage

The last thing that I wish to discuss in this chapter is the matter of teachers, masters and lineage. I've met with opinions that a Reiki lineage is something pointless and useless, or even something that is merely embracing the teacher's ego. But as it turns out, quite often it is the lineage that can tells us what kind of teacher we're dealing with.

Sogyal Rinpoche says:

> People who encounter the Tibetan Buddhism for the first time, wonder often why do we embrace the matter of lineage so greatly. Well, this lineage is one of the greatest insurance that we have, that insure the authenticity and clarity of the teachings. People know who is their teacher, by knowing the teacher's teacher. Thus, it's not about prevailing so old archaic ritual traditions, but about the teachings that come from heart to heart, from mind to mind, originating from the pure wisdom and effective teachings associated with it.[25]

I wish to point out an interesting detail – often, on the lineage

---

25 Ibidem (author's translation)

some names can be lost and forgotten many years after the lineage was continued by the teacher's students. Often, the practices can be lost and recreated over time. It's worth to look what kind of practices were lost by whom and what practices were rediscovered by whom. The lineage is a story of ups and downs, the journey towards enlightenment, during which every teacher has added something on his own. Such lineage shows what teachers did in the past – some got rid of things, some added things, and others repaired things.

This leads us to another issue – who is a Reiki teacher? Personally, I believe that a teacher is just a normal Reiki practitioner. And this practitioner becomes a teacher only for a time necessary to teach someone else and share the knowledge. If he or she is not running a class or workshop, the the person should act like a normal, ordinary Reiki practitioner. The person should be friendly, nice and helpful, even if he or she is not a perfect spiritual master – and many of Reiki teachers are not really spiritual masters, even if they share the Reiki knowledge in professional way.

One of the Healing Tao teachers, Roman Fierfas, said once during one of his lectures:

> The role of the teacher is not to pass the power. The role of the teacher is to help the student discover the power that the student already has inside.

This is how the Reiki teacher should act – he should be showing, in a friendly way, to others the ways how people can discover the power on their own, a power they already have inside of them. And what about Reiki „masters"? This is even simpler. Despite the amount of titles on the certificates, in reality there is only one master – it's Reiki. And there's only one student – it's you. There is nothing else.

Spiritual and Historical Sources of the Reiki Practice

In this chapter I wish to discuss some (possible) sources of the Reiki practice that can be found in Buddhism, Shinto and Taoism. In addition, I will discuss some basic concepts that originate from these schools of spiritual thought, that are associated with Reiki, one way or another. I will discuss the basic ideas and historical aspects – more of these will be present in the following chapters.

From Buddha to Usui

In order to understand the practice of Reiki better, we should explore the roots of this method – where does it come from, who was its creator, where did all these associations with Buddhism or

Shinto come from and so on. Of course, the method of Reiki, historically speaking, was created at the beginning of the XX century, there's no doubt about this. Also, we cannot say that Reiki is a Buddhist practice, because that wouldn't be true. Reiki is not a Buddhist practice, it merely refers to the Buddhist ideals, and the roots of some Reiki practices can be found in Buddhism. The same thing goes for Shinto and Taoism. Reiki refers to the ideals of both Shinto and Taoism, and in both of these ideologies the roots of some Reiki practices can be found, but these practices themselves have been created by Usui himself.

Also, we need to set a difference between the Reiki energy and the Reiki method. The energy, or „force" itself is definitely far older than the method of working with the energy itself. But the method, known as Usui Shiki Ryoho Reiki, a collection of theoretical knowledge and practical techniques, is about 100 years old, and it's a historical fact. As created by Usui Mikao, it took its traditional shape between 1910-1926.

That said, the roots of this method – that means the archetypes of some practices, the archetypes of theory, reach deep into the history of the World. In order to understand this better and begin this chapter, we must go back for about 2500 years in time, to the age when Buddhism was born.

The Influence of Buddhism

The historical Buddha, Sidharta Gautama, after he experienced his enlightenment, started to share his teachings. Based on these teachings, the first Buddhism school was created, the school of Theravada („Doctrine of the Elders"), that was later named Hinayana. This school of thought moved East – today, it's one of the main two schools of Buddhism. Its influence over the Reiki practice is probably none at all. The teachings that reached Japan were part of a different school, the Mahayana Buddhism, the Buddhism of the Great Vehicle. This school moved from present India, the place where Buddha was born, and traveled North-East, to Tibet, and then to China.[26] The Mahayana Buddhism guards the belief that enlightenment is not a benefit meant for a single person, but it's a benefit for all mankind.

In some way, because Usui was a Buddhist of a Mahayana school, and as some sources say he may have been a lay monk, this ideal of "enlightenment for all mankind" was kept strongly in his heart when he created the method of Reiki. Thus, it's worth to remember that working with Reiki, even if it's a practice of self-healing, should be performed in such way that the results will benefit all living and feeling beings – which is a manifestation of the Mahayana ideals.

In the Mahayana school, there is a concept of Bodhisattva – the enlightened beings that decided to remain on Earth in their spiritual form, for the sole purpose of helping other living begins in reaching enlightenment. These beings declared that they will not leave our planes of existence unless all beings break away from the wheel of death and reborn (Samsara). What is interesting is that some Bodhisattvas, through the Reiki symbols, are somehow associated with the Reiki practice. But this will be discussed later on.

Part of the Mahayana Buddhism is the Tantra Buddhism, that is also known as the Esoteric Buddhism. It is focused on rituals and the inner energy (it's an oversimplification of things, but it will have to do for the purpose of this book). This Esoteric Buddhism includes practice of working with symbols, mantras and mandalas.[27] This ideology is focused on the process of

---

26 Williams, P., *Buddyzm Mahajana*, p. 102.

27 Ibidem

transforming the reality and the inner selfs of all practitioners, for the sole purpose of bettering the way the practitioners can help other living beings.

The mikkyo teachings are the esoteric Buddhism's teachings in Japan – they are commonly practiced in the schools of tantra Buddhism in Japan, the Tendai and Shingon – in other words, the mikkyo teachings are the esoteric teachings. While in the West, the tantra teachings are too often associated only with sexual practices, in reality this is a simplification of things. In its primal meaning, the tantra Buddhism is an egalitarian practice, in which through the use of special practices that improve the body and mind, the practitioner is capable of understanding and experiencing the Highest Truth. What is interesting is that tantra Buddhism believes in the idea that all that exists is a result of the interaction and connection of the male and female elements, known as Yin and Yang, or In and Yo in Japan.[28] This will prove interesting later when we discuss the two of three diamonds.

Let's go back to the path of Buddhism leading from India to Japan. From China, thanks to two monks known as Kukai and Saicho, the esoteric Buddhism traveled to Japan after year 803 of our age. Also, other schools of Buddhism traveled to Japan due to activity of other monks, some of them from China, others from Korea. For example, a famous school of Japanese Buddhism called Zen evolved from the Chinese Buddhism of Chan.[29] The school of Pure Land Buddhism (Jodo Shu) evolved from the esoteric Buddhism of Tendai mainly due to the works of monks Honen and Shinran. Other schools of Buddhism in Japan are Kegon[30], and of course the two schools already mentioned – the Tendai, created by

---

28 Jakimowicz, A., Jakimowicz-Shah, M., *Mitologia indyjska*, p. 360-361.

29 Williams, P., *Buddyzm Mahajana*, p. 142.

30 Ibidem

Saicho, and Shingon, created by Kukai. Both of these schools are referred to with the term of Mikkyo – the inner teachings, the secret teachings or the esoteric teachings. The creators of the schools Tendai, Shingon and Jodo Shu, also helped the evolving interaction with the home religion of Shinto.[31]

Because of the cultural aspects, the Buddhism of Mahayana connected itself with the state religion of Shinto, connecting together not only the rituals, but also the spiritual beings in an eclectic way. The entities that interest us from our Reiki perspective are the Nyorai and the Bosatsu – those are the terms that define the types of entities. The Nyorai is the Japanese term for the primal Buddhas – powerful spiritual and enlightened beings, that cannot interact with people directly. That is why, from their compassion, the Bosatsu were born. It's a Japanese term for Bodhisattva, the enlightened beings that work for the highest good of all living beings. Two of the Nyorai are associated with Reiki – it's the Dainichi Nyorai (the Vairocana Buddha, eclectically equal to the Shinto deity of Amaterasu[32]) and the Amida Nyorai (the Amithaba Buddha). Two of Bodhisattvas are associated with Reiki. It's the Kannon, known also as Kanzeon Bosatsu (Bodhisattva Avalokiteśvara) and Daiseishi Bosatsu (Bodhisattva Mahasthamaprapta). These entities along with their symbolic meaning will be discussed later in this book.

The creator of Reiki, Usui Mikao, was a practitioner of the Jodo Shu Buddhism, the Pure Land Buddhism. Because of this, he is buried on the cemetery next to the Jodo Shu temple. Because his clan was closely associated with this school, Usui was well educated in the main deity of this school, the Amida Buddha and the symbol that represents this Buddha – the second Reiki symbol

---

31 Tubielewicz, J., *Mitologia Japonii*, p. 17.

32 Hall, J.W., *Japonia od czasów najdawniejszych do dzisiaj*, p. 68.

of SHK. I will discuss both this Buddha and the symbol later. Usui Mikao attended a school next to a temple in Taniai, and this is where he started his spiritual studies, that later on lead him to become familiar with the schools of Mikkyo – the Tendai and Shingon. Later on, his journey took him further into Shinto and the ascetic practices of Shugendo.

The practice of Reiki refers to the Buddhism of Mahayana, and the primary idea of this school is the ideal of Bodhisattva. The common characteristic of these beings, and all the people who walk the path of Bodhisattva, is the ideal of Wisdom (Sanskrit: Prajna) and Compassion (Sanskrit: Karuna). This second ideal can be seen in the Reiki precept: *hito ni shinsetsu ni*, that translates as „just for today, be compassionate to all living beings". The context of this precept is clear: act with compassion directed to all that exists and feel.

Following the ideals of the esoteric Buddhism, the practice of Reiki suggests the inner transformations of self, of every single practitioner as individual, but also the transformation of the reality surrounding us, so that we can work better for the benefit of all living beings. Following this thought, it may also suggest an honest work, vegetarianism, care of the environment and ecology, but also the improvement of the inner ethics, or the ability of empathy and development of the skill to support all living beings.

To say more, the school of Jodo Shu is the school of Mahayana Buddhism. Another characteristic of this path is its simplicity and availability when compared to a more difficult path of Hinayana. An author and scholar named Tubielewicz writes that Mahayana is „a path that is far more available to the general public".[33] This is another thing that may have influenced Usui, so that he was able to create the system of Reiki in such way that it became available and

---

33 Tubielewicz, J., *Mitologia Japonii*, p. 11.

easy to practice to ordinary people (ordinary, meaning those who lived a normal life instead of a monastery life).

We should notice that Buddhism is often called „the Middle Path". On the road to happiness and freeing from suffering, Buddhism do not suggest asceticism nor unnecessary richness. It suggest walking the middle path, when we live a simple life, when we have enough goods for ourselves and we're happy to share with others. Similar to this, Reiki do not suggest asceticism nor it suggests an over-splendor life. It leads to a peaceful, honorable life full of wealth, a life in which we nevertheless known when enough is enough and we're happy to share our richness and happiness.

To summarize, we may say that Buddhism influenced Reiki through the method's creator, Usui Mikao, who was a Buddhist of a Pure Land school. This school can be characterized with simplicity and great availability to ordinary folks. This simplicity and availability is seen in the method of Reiki, a method that can be learned by every person. Reiki was also influenced by the Mikkyo teachings that explored the integration of the three diamonds (the Yin, the Yang and the diamond of Heart) through the work with symbols, mantras and the energy itself. And finally, Buddhism influenced Reiki by transferring into Reiki its ideals of peace, serenity and middle way through compassion and wisdom.

The Influence of Shinto and Shugendo

The Mahayana Buddhism can be characterized by another fact — it easily integrates itself with local traditions. This was the case in any place where this school of Buddhist thought came to.[34] That said, in Japan, for example, the great Dainichi Nyorai was identified with the Sun goddess Amaterasu, the most important deity in the Shinto religion.[35] Buddhism is connected to Shinto also

34 Williams, P., *Buddyzm Mahajana*, p. 231.
35 Ibidem

due to the teachings of Dogen and other Buddhist teachers who said that all that exists in nature has Buddha's nature. This was closely connected to the traditional Japanese view upon the nature and environment,[36] that in itself was and still is sacred. This point of view is a result of the fact that Shinto is an animistic religion, in which we deal with so called Kami – the spiritual beings, that were somehow turned into deities, and they're the „spirits" of rocks, rivers, lakes, mountains, trees, homes or caves – of all that is.

This spiritual, animistic perspective is clear in Reiki in the deep respect for all living beings, and to all that exists, as well. This is closely associated with Reiki. The practice opens the practitioner to an awareness of sacredness of the world that surrounds us. The practice also motivates us to take care of Mother Nature and the environment. This awareness and this perspective arrives on its own, as a result of practice, and makes us understand that we are all children of the Earth and we should take care for our home.

What are other ways of how Shinto influenced the practice of Reiki? We need to definitely mentioned the Shinto practice of Shugendo. To describe it simply, Shugendo is a form of Shinto magick, but it should be understood as a mixture of Shinto, Taoist and Buddhist teachings. The practitioners of Shugendo are called Yamabushi or Shugenja. They chose ascetic practices they perform in the mountains, by using mantras and symbols for the purpose of healing.[37] It is said that Usui, as he was practicing in the mountains, met with Yamabushi and received teachings from them, and this influenced the Reiki practice as well. Shugendo influenced the esoteric practices of Tendai and Shingon as well.

The very journey of Usui that he made by climbing the Kurama

---

36 Ibidem

37 Stiene, B., Stiene F., *Japanese Art of Reiki*, p. 10-12.

Yama carries a lot of signs associated with Shinto and Shugendo. First of all, the Kurama Yama itself was popular among the Yamabushi, and second of all, the mountains themselves were considered in Japan to be the places of great spiritual power. The mountains were places where temples were build, and the cities or villages were placed in the valleys or in the lowlands. Shugendo is the path of spiritual power as achieved through individual practice, closely related not just with Shinto, but also with Buddhism. In the past it was common to say that Shugendo is a form of folk Buddhist practice.[38]

To summarize, the influence of Shinto and Shugendo over Reiki is seen mainly in the use of symbols and mantras for the purpose of healing. The Shugendo practitioners also worked with comic powers and they understood the depth of the personal, individual practice. Beside that, Shugendo and Shinto's influence can be seen in the mere fact that Usui knew to seek spiritual power in the mountains.

The Influence of Taoism

The last of the great schools of thought that influenced Reiki is the Chinese Taoism. There are two primary schools of Taoism – to simplify the description. The first version of Taoism is the ideology, and the second Taoism is the religion. The first one, the ideological version of Taoism, along with its esoteric and philosophical thought, influenced the evolution of Buddhism itself.

When Buddhism reached China, a lot of terms and concepts Buddhist in origin were being explained through Taoist terminology. This traditional Chinese terms sometimes simplified and sometimes complicated the understanding of Buddhist concepts.[39] Taoism influenced greatly the evolution of Buddhism in

---

38 Lubeck, W., Hosak, M., *The Big Book of Reiki Symbols*, p. 136.
39 Williams, P., *Buddyzm Mahajana*, p. 150.

China, but it also traveled to Japan where a lot of elements were transfered, as well. Taoism influenced the school of Zen and other schools of Buddhism. Some traditional Taoist practices reached Japan as well, and they have been probably used by Usui to assign the Reiki symbols to the method itself. Another concept influenced by Taoism is the dualistic perspective upon reality – the Chinese Yin and Yang changed into Japanese In and Yo – in this concept we recognize the two of three diamonds – the earthly diamond and the heavenly diamond.[40] The concept of Yin and Yang will be discussed later in this book, but for now I just explain that the taoists believed that everything that exists is a result of interaction between the energies of earth and heaven – the energies of Yin and Yang. Those two elements are the great parents of everything that exists.[41] In the context of the Reiki practice we understand Yin as earth energies and Yang as the heaven energies.

Taoism also influenced the popularity of ascetic practices in Japan,[42] and most probably through this it influenced the practices of Shugendo.

Lubeck and Hosak suggests that the concept of Dao (Tao) – the Source – also influenced the spiritual culture of Japan, and through this, the very idea of Reiki. The Dao is the Source, from which everything originates and into which everything returns. Tao is represented by the harmonious interaction of Yin and Yang.[43]

***

---

40 Tubielewicz, J., *Mitologia Japonii*, p. 8.

41 Ibidem, p. 8

42 Ibidem, p. 8

43 Lubeck, W., Hosak, M., *The Big Book of Reiki Symbols*, p. 121-122.

Different ideals and concepts of the Japanese culture can be spotted in the practice of Reiki. But in its essence, these ideals and concepts can be simplified to the basic idea of reaching the state of unity and returning to the Source (Dao) through the individual practice that is meant to integrate the Yin and Yang and bring harmony to these two elements. Now we have learned the roots of the explained concepts, and their practical effects will be explained shortly. Just before we do so, some additional concepts related to Reiki should be discussed.

Spiritual Ideas and Concepts in Reiki

Now that we have discussed the influence of the great ideologies of Buddhism, Taoism and Shinto on the development of Reiki, it's worth discussing some concepts and ideals of ethics and spirituality, that are somehow related to the practice of Reiki, and which we can discover in the Five Precepts (Gokai). These precepts should not be merely a guideline that shows the practitioner the direction to blindly follow. They should show you a real spiritual goal that is worth of reaching, so that you can understand the spiritual concepts yourself. In result, every person can develop spiritually like he or she is meant to.

Let's recall the main part of the Reiki Precepts.

> For today only:
> Do not anger
> Do not worry
> Be humble
> Be honest in your work
> Be compassionate to yourself and others.[44]

---

44 Chris Marsh translation.

To these precepts we may relate some of the ideals of the Japanese culture, that will be discussed now. Three main concepts are important for the practice of Reiki, and they originate from Buddhism. These are Kaji, Compassion and Wisdom.

Kaji

Kaji is not a simple concept, but in its basic, yet partial understanding, we may say that Kaji is an honest intention of growth (self-healing). A Buddhist seeks refuge in the three jewels: Buddha, his Dharma (teachings) and Sangha, the spiritual community. „Taking refuge" should be properly understood – it's a strong intention of taking a spiritual journey in accordance with the ideas of Buddhism. It's a decision to walk the spiritual path despite the difficulties that may be encountered on this path – this is the intention of Kaji, an honest wish to act honestly to yourself, others and the entire world. Kaji is not an energy, it's a factor. It's a spiritual force that helps us on our spiritual journey if our intentions are true and honest.

The Reiki practitioner, if he or she wish to work successful with this method, must surrender to Kaji. To be clear, it is not a connection with some spirits or entities or groups of people, no. Kaji is your very own intention of changing your life for better. It's an intention of being a better person, of healing, or helping, or being a good person for yourself and everything that surrounds you. And this intention has to be kept clear in our mind. As we practice and as we live our life day by day, as Reiki practitioners we must be constantly aware why do we practice and what is important in life. This is where we discover the ideas like ethics, honest work, tolerance, helping fellow beings and taking care of everything that exists.

In a way, this concept integrates with the idea of Jungian synchronicity. A synchronicity, as promoted by jungians, is an occurrence when so called „coincidences" turns out to have a much deeper meaning. On the path of Reiki this is clearly and often visible. We ask a question, and the answer comes to us after some time in form of an inspiring book, discussion or song on the radio. Or sometimes, we need help, and this help comes to us in the most unexpected moment. Or we seek something, and we find it when we have already lost hope to find it. Most people say these are coincidences. The jungians say it's synchronicity. And people interested in New Age will say that those are spiritual forces or the law of attraction in motion.

But Reiki practitioner will say that it's Kaji – our intention was honest, so the spiritual power acted on it, so that we can receive the answer or get that what we really need at the moment.

This intention and this force of Kaji, manifests on many levels – for example, it manifests between the teacher and the student. The teacher honestly wishes self-healing for the student – thus, the Kaji will guide the student on his or hers own path to healing. Kaji manifests between the Reiki practitioner and the receiver of Reiki treatment. The practitioner wishes for the person to be honestly healed, and this is when Kaji works. But the most important intention is one one the practitioner feels towards himself or herself – the self-intention of healing.

The practitioner needs to honestly wish to be healed and the practitioner must honestly grow spiritually. And this intention must be kept in mind all the time, and when the practitioner strays from the spiritual path, then he must return to the primary, honest intention of healing. When this intention is honest and true, when the practitioner truly wish to grow and self-heal, then despite falls and downs on the path of growth, Reiki will keep leading the person to the state of unity and harmony and rediscovery of the primal Buddha's nature.

Kaji makes it unnecessary to constantly seek answers. We just define our honest intention, we work with Reiki and we live by the Five Precepts and in result that which we need – people, books, techniques, answers and inspirations – will find us on their own, sooner or later. And it doesn't matter if we're talking about finding a good job, finding true love or actually achieving the final enlightenment. If we make no harm to other living beings, then both Reiki and Kaji will work to our benefit.

Compassion

The Buddhist idea of Compassion is not easy to understood, but it definitely has nothing in common with feeling pity over someone. At the same time, it's not about the kind of compassion when we accept the pain and suffering of others as our own pain and suffering, so that we can clear their „karma" through our meditations. Compassion is about honest care and will to help all living beings while remaining aware that we're all in it together – we all experience pain and suffering, both emotional and physical.

While the idea of Compassion in Buddhism itself is very complicated, in the context of Reiki I usually teach something like this. Try to feel and think like the other person – try to imagine what the life of this other person looks like. When someone acts bad towards you or others, do not judge. The fundamental aspect of Compassion is the ability to understand and constant awareness of the fact that the reason for bad behavior is the pain others experience. The person that is mean to us, for example, may have his or hers problems, problems that we never even dreamed of.

But sometimes, it's just that someone behaves in wrong way, because he have all the reasons to do so. He carries the pain, experience problems back at home, or in love, he can't get over them. By developing our compassion, we learn to see this and understand this. No longer a bad person stands in front of us – instead, we see a person that is lost in the world of personal problems. As we become aware of this, it becomes much easier for us to relate to this person, and even help the person, no matter how this person acts.

One of the elements of the Reiki method is the practice of treatments when we channel spiritual energy to other people or living beings in general. These treatments should originate in our sense of Compassion: that is, from our awareness that the other person has a life, too – family, hobbies, passions and problems, too. This person experience happiness and pain just as we do, and our task – as Reiki practitioners - is to honestly help this person in embracing happiness and healing the pain.

While it's not a concept of true Buddhist Compassion, it is recommended to constantly remember that the bad behavior of others is always caused by something in the life of those people. This ability to remember the fact helps us understand others and help them at the same time.

This Compassion, as we develop our Reiki practice, will grow and develop on many different layers. From this Compassion, for example, personal decision to go vegan may develop. Or a decision to change the job for a more honest one, or to developer healthier relations with people. Things like this may happen. Remember the words of Dalailama:

> [Compassion] should find its place in our hearts, like it's chained there. This Compassion is not interested with only a few living beings, like friends or relatives, but it reaches the far ends of the Universe, in all directions, to all living

beings everyone out there.[45]

To all living beings everywhere out there – this is the greatest Compassion. Compassion is also related to the idea of the highest good of all living beings. This idea, that Reiki acts in accordance with the highest good, should be kept in your heart and mind all the time, whenever you do Reiki to yourself or others.

Know that sometimes our heart screams „I hate!" When this happens, remember that it's just a minor setback. What you should pay attention to is not the hate towards someone, but that which lies under it, that which is hidden behind the pain. That which is hidden in the unconscious mind must be healed, and then all the experience of hate will be just another experience to help you change your life for better. Sometimes people experience pain because they tripped on their spiritual path – they cursed, they got angry, destroyed everything they were building for so many years. But do not fall into this trap of pain. Every single setback on the path of spiritual grow is merely a sign that you have something new to heal. It's just another thing that must be taken care of. Just another experience to learn from. Keep the Kaji in your heart – the true and pure intention of growth every single time you trip, and then your life and Reiki will guide you further and further, and you won't be afraid of anything.

Wisdom

Another ideal and concept that comes important on the path of Reiki is wisdom. Wisdom is not the same thing as intelligence. Wisdom, from the Buddhist perspective, is the state of full understanding, the ability to see the difference between the reality and the illusion, by experiencing the insights into the nature of

---

45 Williams, P., *Buddyzm Mahajana*, p. 243.

reality – this develops along with the spiritual practice and meditation. We begin to see the difference between that which is merely an illusion created by our mind and that which is the true nature of the reality. For the Reiki practitioner, it starts by learning the mechanisms and actions that create specific results, and learning the truths that we find behind that which we experience every single day. This beginner's aspect is what interests us in this book.

Wisdom makes us stop worry, because we see that from stillness and peace and regular practice and healing we create good, peaceful life, in which we don't have to be afraid. We give up anger, because we begin to see the reasons for getting angry and we can use this ability to improve ourselves.

When Kaji is at work, we flow with Dao, and things happen on their own. When we act with Compassion, we act for the goodness of all living beings, for all that is. When we devote ourselves to the practice of Reiki, either through self-treatment, or through meditations, and we integrate the Five Precepts into our life, we gain peace and we begin to recognize that which causes our experiences. We begin to understand our past actions, and our pains and experiences, or beliefs taken for granted from others – and all of these things shape our life.

From that, our understanding is born – the understanding that the unconscious shapes our life and motivates our actions. From that on, we develop the ability to heal that which is unconscious, hidden in the subconscious mind, and this helps us release ourselves from the control of the unconscious. From that, the first sparkles of Wisdom are born, and thanks to Wisdom, we begin to understand that whatever happens, we can find the source of this inside ourselves. From this Wisdom, inner peace is born, too, along with the awareness that whatever happens, we can deal with it.

*****

We have discussed the roots of the practice of Reiki, and some important spiritual concepts, that you may experience on the path of Reiki. I'm sure that it is just one small part of the deeper knowledge. But understanding these aspects further would require us to deepen our understanding of Buddhism through detailed studies, and this is not the goal of this book. For now, we can move on and explain, finally, what are the Three Diamonds in the practice of Reiki, and why are they important for the Reiki practitioner.

The Way of Three Diamonds

Now that we have discussed the basic theory, that is important to understand more advanced aspects of Reiki, we can discuss what are the Three Diamonds, where do they come from and why is it important to understand them in order to understand the practice of Reiki.

To satisfy the facts, it must be stated that the concept of the Three Diamonds and the Five Elements of Reiki practice is a modern creation that has been introduced into the world of Reiki by Bronwen and Frans Stiene, Reiki teachers from Australia. For many years they were researching the historical and spiritual background of the Usui Shiki Ryoho Reiki. Frans Stiene studied Buddhism, Taoism and Shinto, along with the arts of Shugendo, and from his research, our understanding of the Three Diamonds is born.

According to Stiene, it is quite possible that Mikao Usui, who was a lay monk as far as we know, knowledgeable of the Shingon and Tendai schools of Buddhism,[46] was also familiar with the path of Shugendo, thus the concept of Three Diamonds must have been familiar to him, as well.

Stiene's research seems to be logical and puts the entire practice of Reiki in new light. From this modern knowledge we know that the path of Reiki is a very complex and spiritually deep practice, most of which has been forgotten in the "Western" versions that often limits Reiki to a healing practice. Let's get deeper into the path of Reiki, then...

According to Stiene, the following traditions influenced the path of Reiki:

1. **Mikkyo teachings** – these teachings originate from the Buddhism school of Tendai, based on the Lotus Sutra,[47] that is said to contain the complete and final teachings of the Buddha. Mikkyo teachings influenced mainly the practice with jumons (the sounds of the symbols) and the symbols themselves, as well as the practice with esoteric, „inner" teachings of Reiki.

2. **Shinto** – this Japanese animistic[48] religion influenced the way of perceiving the world and the way the energy works. Also, it influenced the practice of healing through laying on of hands.

3. **Martial arts** – these influenced the concept of Ki energy

---

46 Stiene, B., Stiene F., *Japanese Art of Reiki*, p. 8.

47 Lotus Sutra is considered to be a text of great spiritual power, and it's also associated with the school of Jodu Shu, the Pure Land.

48 **Animism** – a common name for spiritual or religious practices of the primal people, tribes or natives, that were observed in many parts of the World.

and working with breathing techniques.

4. **Shugendo** – an ancient practice of ascetic mountain monks, that integrates together the paths of Buddhism, Taoism and Shinto, which influenced the spiritual understanding of most of the spiritual traditions of Japan.

While the ideologies, paths and traditions mentioned above influenced the practice of Reiki, Mikao Usui managed to cut off the practice from them and made it stand alone. That is why modern Reiki is both independent from other religions and ideologies. Reiki has its roots in the mentioned paths, because Usui used the knowledge and practices from these paths in order to create a completely new system of spiritual healing – the Usui Shiki Ryoho Reiki.

Reiki – The Path that Leads to Unity

Lao Tsu said:

> If you are depressed you are living in the past.
> If you are anxious you are living in the future.
> If you are at peace you are living in the present.

The ability to be here and now and the feeling of inner peace are both signs that we live in the state of Unity. We said already that Reiki is the path that leads to harmony and balance. We may also say that Reiki is the path that leads us to achieving the state of unity – unity with ourselves and with the world around us. We should take a look at the table below to understand better the idea of unity.

Unity	Separation
Patience	Impatience
Peace	Worries, fears
Acceptance	Lack of Acceptance
Going with Life	Chaos, fighting life
Tolerance	Hate
Dialogue	Fight
Inner richness	Inner emptiness
Trust	Lack of trust
Respecting nature	Exploiting nature

The man of the West can be categorized as a person suffering from separation. He fights with life, he is inpatient, hateful and is afraid of other people, or afraid of the future, he cannot learn how to trust. Reiki helps in regaining the state of harmony. Reiki teaches patience, trust for life and other people, tolerance and dialog instead of fighting. All of this happens with the help of Five Elements (treatments, meditations, precepts etc.), that helps us heal our inner Shadow (fears, bad emotions, wrong behaviors) and develop our virtues and talents (happiness, love, compassion). Reiki helps us live a healthier life and care of the Mother Nature, it gives us inner strength and inner peace.

Reiki helps us regain peace and connection with spirituality in the chaotic world. Reiki helps us find ourselves anew. Each practice, each breath, each self-treatment and every single crisis and fall on the path of spiritual healing is another step that gets us closer to the state of unity and finding our inner peace. This is the greatest goal of the regular Reiki practice.

Some of you will ask – so where is this promise of perfect physical health, that is promised on so many Reiki workshops? Well, health manifests with time. As we progress towards the state of harmony, our health improves. Reiki class cannot make guarantees that we stop getting ill. It guarantees that we will be able to work with Reiki, and the practice of this method, with time, will improve our health more and more: less things will ache us, our immune system will get stronger and after many years of practice, illnesses will be merely something in the past.

The state of Unity and health manifests with the progressing practice of Reiki.

The Concept of Three Diamonds

According to spiritual teachings in Japan, a result of Buddhism, Taoism and Shinto co-existing with each other, it is said that the path towards enlightenment becomes open once the two Diamonds are integrated together – the Diamond of Earth force, and the Diamond of Heaven force. From this integration, the third Diamond is born, the Diamond of the Heart – the essence of humanity, the energy of pure and real love, real compassion that awakens the inner awareness of Buddha's nature. Through such integration, a force is activated, a force, thanks to which in Buddhism we say that every living being has a potential for enlightenment. **Reiki is the path of Three Diamonds.**

The practice of Reiki leads to developing the Earth force (energy) within us (Diamond of Earth), Heaven energy (emotional-mental energy, Diamond of Heaven) and integrate them together in order to return us to our primal nature, out Buddha's nature (the Diamond of the Heart, the energy of the heart).

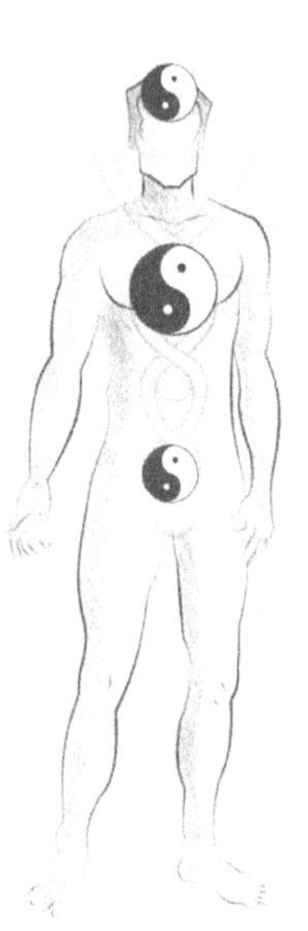

These are the locations of the three Dantiens in the body. The first Dantien, Hara, is placed in the abdomen. The second dantien is placed in the heart, and the third dantien is placed in the head. Between them, according to Taoism teachings, there are two primary energy channels connecting the dantiens together – the front and back channel. Together they create what is called the microcosmic orbit.

The Three Diamonds mentioned are mirrored in the physical realm – their representations are placed within the human body in three places: in the abdomen (Hara region), in the heart and in the head – exactly in the places pointed out by Taoism teachings, originating in China. It's not that strange – Buddhism and a lot of Japanese culture reached Japan due to the contact with the mainland China, as it was mentioned earlier in this book. These three regions in the body are the Three Dantiens – the energetic centers, as we can call them to simplify things.

According to Taoist teachings it is said that we should never work directly with the second and third dantien. We can work safely only with the first dantien, the Hara. But these dantiens are connected with each other. When the first dantien is activated fully, the spiritual energy goes to the second dantien, and once this one is full and activated, the energy reaches the third dantien.

Nevertheless, on the path of Reiki we work directly only with the first dantien, the region of Hara in the abdomen. In a passive way, the second dantien benefits from meditations, breathing techniques and working with the Gassho mudra, and the third dantien benefits from the general practice.

A Buddhist mudra „Gassho" - hands together.

It is worth to mention that Mikao Usui could or could have been not familiar with the concept of Chakras. Either way, there are no proofs that he used this knowledge (if any) in his system of Reiki. Often, in Chujiro Hayashi's notes, or in the teachings of Usui Reiki

Ryoho Gakkai, or in the notes of Hawayo Takata, we can clearly see that one of the most important elements of Reiki is the concept of dantiens.

Three Diamonds and the Reality

Reiki practitioner who do not walk the path of Three Diamonds will never experience full healing. But, it's interesting that this path is walked also by those practitioners who merely practice self-treatment and do not worry about any deeper understanding of Reiki. In order to understand this, we should relate the Three Diamonds to the physical reality and the daily life. First, let's take a look at the following table, so we won't get lost in translation.

Diamond	Chinese	Japanese	Energy
Earth Diamond	Yin	In	Earth Energy
Heaven Diamond	Yang	Yo	Heaven Energy
Heart Diamond	-	-	Heart Energy

The above are the different terms for the same thing – for example, when we speak about the Diamond of Earth, at the same time we understand it as the influence of the Earth energy, and the entire concept of Yin (Chinese) or In (Japanese).

We should mention the idea of Taoist concepts of Yin and Yang. Jou Tsung Hwa says:

> Generally speaking, Yin and Yang are the opposite forces that complement each other, creating a harmonious whole. Though their natures are opposite, they exist in a harmonious relations. (...) Yang is heat, movement,

activity, and Yin is cold, stillness, lack of activity.[49]

The symbols Yin and Yang have many different meanings – they are opposite to each other, like day and night, good and evil. But only together they create harmonious whole. We will never be happy with the warm weather of Summer, if we won't experience the cold of Winter. And we must remember that it is in the nature of things that Winter comes after Summer, and Summer comes after Winter. This is the nature of things, this is Dao, the Way. In this philosophy, we can find many useful tips for the practice of Reiki.

For example, lack of harmony between Yin and Yang leads to inability to create – from this, destruction is made. Only when we reach the state of harmony between Yin and Yang, we can create, we can live in accordance with the Dao – flow with the great river of life. Only then, we recognize our natural talents and strengths (Yang), thanks to which we can act without effort. We recognize our weaknesses and problems (Yin) and accept them, so that they won't interfere with out life from the subconscious.

We learn, too, that sometimes the Yin is needed, to destroy the old structures, so what we can build new Yang above it. Further on, we learn that sometimes we live in the state of Yang – we have a lot of strength, happiness, motivation and we want to act on it. But it is normal that after some time, Yin will take the wheel, we we will prefer to sit down, still and peaceful, and we won't have the need to act. It is the nature of our life to experience the great cycles of active and passive, of giving and taking, pushing forwards and pulling back.

The symbols Yin and Yang themselves, at the very beginning, used to symbolize the two slopes of the mountain, one filled with

---

49 Hwa, J. T., *Droga Tai Chi*, p. 106-107.

sunlight, the other one hidden in shadows – these opposite slopes never fought with each other, they co-existed together in harmony. They existed thanks to the infinite source of energy – the Sun.[50] In the same way, in the practice of Reiki the Diamonds of Earth and Heaven – the Yin and Yang (In and Yo), exist together, despite their differences. They exist thanks to the primal source of energy.

When we understand our own inner Yang and Yin, and the way these energies manifest in our life, we begin to experience the state of harmony, unity, and the path of Reiki will result in success. In order to achieve this, we must practice. We must integrate our light side with our dark side, Yang with Yin. By merging the two opposite things, like hobby with job, relaxation with duty – we direct ourselves towards the state of inner harmony. The integration of the elements of Heaven and Earth (Yang and Yin) leads us to achieving the state of inner harmony not by the physical energy work, like in case of Qigong, for example, but by calm and peaceful inner work with the highest form of spiritual energy available to an ordinary person.

The Yin and Yang forces are also related to the Diamonds in the practice of Reiki. The Three Diamonds can be seen in all three Reiki degrees. The first degree, Shoden, is focused on the physical reality. We work with that which is physical, material, but also passive and Yin. The second degree, Okuden, is focused on that which is emotional and Yang. The third degree, Shinpiden, opens our way towards integration of the first two degrees into the daily life.

The first Diamond, the earth energy, is the material world and the layer of Yin. The physical reality is that which is physical: food, drinks, touch, physical intimacy, work and hobby, health and physical activity, all that we can related to the earth forces, whether

---

50 Hansen, C., Toropov, B., *Taoizm dla żółtodziobów*, p. 65

it's Mother Nature, high income or good relations with other people. Working with this Diamond is manifested in the life of the practitioner on many layers.

It's working with this Diamond that makes our habits and lifestyle change – we change our diet for a more healthy one, we give up coffee, alcohol or at least limit them. We change our job, we find our passions and interests for hobbies. We develop our talents and natural abilities that can be changed into physical safety. We change our relations, we give up people what are no longer good for us. We fight with toxins in our body, and we start doing sport. Here is also where we find the strength to decrease the amount of stress and worries, that weaken our immune system.

On the other hand, the layer of Yin can be described with words such as: female, passive, darkness, submission.[51] The first degree of Reiki may need us to deal with these aspects of our life and personality, that which is related to female energies within us, our Anima – the female aspect of our psyche. The Shoden degree may push us towards contemplation upon the state of passiveness and observation, for example by developing our ability to meditate. Shoden may teach us how to let go of things and flow with life. By doing so, we may awake our talents and inner genius. Shoden is also about our direct connection with Earth – our Great Mother.

The second Diamond is the emotional realm – our feelings and emotions, our points of view and perception of life, the Shadows hidden in the unconscious mind. Those are the scripts of behavior, but also our dreams and goals. It's love and friendship, it's also our need to feel needed and be part of a community, and it's also our need for self-realization. This is what we can call „the heavenly forces". This is also the layer of Yang. This is where the practitioner must heal his traumas, fears and worries. It's also the

---

51 Ibidem, p. 67.

path of changing our behavior and habits, step by step, changing our life style further and defining new goals and priorities.

The Yang can be described with the words such as: male, activity, movement, clarity, creation.[52] The second degree, Okuden, may cause us to focus on the Animus – the male aspect of our psyche. It may push us towards activity, towards achieving our dreams and developing our artistic expression, as we have already learned how to work with our inner peace and passive approach. The second degree develops clarity, and slowly opens our eyes for the sight of nature of reality and reasons why things happen – both as the ability to understand the world around us, and to see the subconscious matrix of our mind that shapes our life. It's also the beginning of our stronger connection with Heaven – associated with God-Creator, higher spiritual power, Great Spirit, or the Source.

The Third Diamond is the energy of the heart, it's the practice of the third degree – Shinpiden. Here we discover nothing more but the practice that leads to integration of the first two Diamonds. This is where we practice in order to integrate together what we have learned in the past. We discover new aspects of the First and Second Diamond, where everything becomes a whole, leading us to the final goal of Unity. We develop compassion, we discover our destiny, we discover our individual spiritual path, and the spiritual truths become clear to us over time. The Diamond of the Heart is discovering the Wu-Chi and Tai-Chi – the emptiness and that which comes from emptiness – words and actions, cause and effect. This is about discovering the Dao, the Way – the source of everything within us and around us.

Perhaps to many readers it becomes clear why Reiki is so effective in healing every aspect of our life by working with, and

---

52 Ibidem, p. 67.

integrating together the Three Diamonds. These are the aspects of Yin and Yang, and the nature of things (Dao) that becomes manifested in our life. By working with Three Diamonds, the body and the mind becomes one. The man reaches the state of Unity with himself and the world around him, and becomes a channel for spiritual force.

Now I want to discuss the meaning of Hara, heart and the head – the physical representations of the Three Diamonds, and – in a way – the three dantiens.

Hara, Heart and Head in the Practice of Reiki

In Chinese culture, the three dantiens are related to the flow of subtle life energy – Chi ("Ki" in Japan). These dantiens, the energy centers, are the representations of the Three Diamonds. On a particular level, by working with the dantiens, we work with each and every Diamond and with everything these Diamonds represent.

And thus, for example, the first dantien, Hara, is associated with the Earth energy, the Diamond of Earth. The second dantien, located in the heart, is associated with the heart energy, the Diamond of the Heart. The third dantien, placed in the head, is associated with the Heaven energy, the Diamond of Heaven. Most practices of Reiki focus on these three symbolic areas of the body.

A lot of modern sources associate the dantiens with energy centers filled with life force. No matter what the sources say about this concept, the practice of Reiki is focused not on the energetic aspect of the dantiens, but on the metaphorical aspect. The Diamonds can be called "energy", but this is not a typical energy from New Age books. It's more like a word that describes a mystical "force" - a factor that make things happen. We should remember this.

And these factors occur in our life when we work with the three dantiens.

The Hara

Hara is located an inch below the navel, an inch or two inside the body. Hara is associated with the very center of a human being, a physical center. It is said that by focusing on Hara, we merge together and connect together the body and the mind. In the practice of Reiki, working with Hara is associated with grounding, Joshin Kokyu Ho meditation, Hatsurei Ho meditation and Seishin Toitsu meditation. Also, reciting the mantras of the Reiki symbols originates from the Hara region.

Most of the meditations mentioned above are breathing techniques. Such meditations were traditionally practiced in both China and Japan, where, for this day, it is believed that the breath (Chi, Ki) carries a life force with it. A lot of breathing techniques in the Far East, related to Taoism and Buddhism, as focused on breathing with your diaphragm, is being practiced in order to bring peace to the mind, but also, to bring out thoughts, beliefs and experiences from the depths of the subconscious mind, so that they can be healed in order to walk forward on the path of spiritual growth.

By merely focusing on the Hara region in the practice of Reiki we achieve something powerful. In the culture of Japan, due to the influence of Buddhism and Taoism, but also thanks to the local beliefs, the abdomen – Hara – is associated with the subconscious mind – the second brain.[53] When we focus our mind on the Hara, then we integrate together the mind with the body. We heal that

---

53 De Martino, R., Fromm, E., Suzuki, D. T., *Buddyzm zen i psychoanaliza*, p. 76-78.

which is unconscious, we open the way for uniting our entire being – which is the goal of Reiki practice. Working with Hara creates a form of passive healing, of which we don't have to be aware. In such passive way, we heal our mind patterns and emotions. But also, if active and aware healing is required, focusing on Hara will bring these thoughts and emotions into the light.

Secondly, by working with the Hara, we develop this region – and that which is related to the Hara. Reiki begins to influence and heal that which we associate with Earth energies, for example, diet, immune system, ways to make money and such. Hara is also the region associated with the „life force management system", Ki or Chi. If this region is strong, then we have a greater will and motivation to live, we're safer financially and we have hope for the future. Also, our immune system and the entire body are stronger.

Working with the Hara offers us the third aspect – we develop our roots, our grounding. By imagining human being as a tree, we see the spiritual growth as development of a great and wonderful upper branches that reach the sky. But only strong and developed roots can assure us that the tree won't fall with such great upper branches. Working with the Hara, especially on the first level of Shoden, as well as working with the first Reiki symbol, the CKR, is like building strong foundation, growing the roots, grounding ourselves. Without proper grounding, no true spiritual path or personal integration is possible.

When our foundation (roots) is strong and solid, when we are well grounded, we can pursuit spiritual growth. We can reach towards healing of our mind (the soul). Thus, we reach the head.

The Head

While Hara is associated with the subconscious mind, the head – associated with another Diamond, the Heaven energy – the head is associated with the mind and soul.[54] Soul is not separated from the mind in the tradition of Japan. Actually, the mind is believed to be a part of the soul.

Mikao Usui said that every illness originates in the mind. Healing the mind results in healing the body, or at least in accepting the irreversible changes to our body. Even from a medical perspective we may agree with that. Emotional fears, worries, bad memories – all of them create tensions in the body that may lead to illness. And sometimes, even healing the negative habits and beliefs allows us to heal the physical body. For example, when we heal the destructive thoughts that push us to eat fast food, so we can change our diet to a healthier one.

In modern Reiki practice, to heal the soul we use mainly so called mental treatment technique, Seiheki Chiryo, that is used to heal bad habits, thoughts, beliefs or opinions that aren't healthy for us, and to heal experiences that have negative influence over our life. But the traditional, regular practice of Reiki method, that is working with the symbols, meditating and other techniques, all of this leads us to accept our emotions and experiences, made peace with the pain of the past and negative beliefs or memories, and to change negative behaviors as well – these are results not of single technique, but of general and regular practice. While the memories or experiences themselves won't disappear, our emotional reaction to them changes. This is what we understand as the process of healing and releasement – when we let things go, when we let go of things that troubled us in the past. By healing and clearing our mind and life like this, we make space for new experiences and new thoughts – this time, thoughts and experiences that are more positive and more beneficial.

Also, simply ny placing our hands on our head and sending Reiki

---

54 Petter, F.A., *This is Reiki*, p. 178.

we gain results in healing our soul. Sending Reiki to the head region heals not just the physical body, but also heals our soul and everything related to our soul – that which is past, present and future. Giving Reiki to the head can be compared to healing the Karma. And by the way, Karma is also related to the heart dantien.

This is the moment when the heart and head dantiens start to interweave with each other and it becomes difficult to see the difference between the two of them. But, after some time you may actually say that it's hard to see a definite difference between any of the dantiens. That's it – all of them interweave with each other, creating a whole. From a Taoist perspective, they're connected with each other and they cannot be discussed as separate beings in the end.

The Heart

The next dantien, the one in the heart, is affected by general meditation practices, but also by the practices like opening to Reiki flow with our hands in Gassho, or by meditating with Gassho Kokyu Ho technique. With Gassho, hands together, we recite the Five Precepts, or the Gokai. This diamond of heart develops as we develop our daily practice.

The diamond of the heart symbolizes a human being opening to the spiritual power, pure intentions of healing and honest intentions of changing the life for better. The heart can be identified with the development of compassion and other spiritual ideals such as wisdom or true love. The heart is healed also by the SHK and HS symbols.

When the mind becomes clearer, and the foundation of the practice gets stronger, then positive spiritual ideals – our spiritual virtues – start to manifest in our life through our Heart. In other words, when we take care of our Hara and our Head diamond, their growth and development will result in growth and development of the Heart. And then, the Reiki practitioner begins to truly feel the spiritual power in his or hers life.

To achieve right spiritual results, we work with different Reiki techniques – and by doing so, we discover and integrate that, which, until now, remained unconscious.

Our True Nature and Integration of the Unconscious

Working with the Tree Diamonds is all about working with our Inner Self. That's why we've reached an important aspect of the Reiki practice – we have to face that which exists within us. Reiki practice is all about looking within ourselves and healing that which we find within us. Kukai, the founder of the Shingon school of Buddhism, said:

> When the medicine of Esoteric teachings have cleared away the dust; True Words open the treasury. When the secret treasures are suddenly displayed:all virtues are apparent.[55]

His esoteric teachings are the teachings of esoteric Buddhism – these teachings are focused on working with the inner self. And this work begins with insight into our own soul, mind and heart. The dust is a symbol of everything that covers and hides the true nature of the mind – the True Words. The nature of the mind, the Buddha's Nature, is out secret treasure, full of many virtues. By practicing Reiki, we clear the dust, so that we can finally see our true, inner virtues. Clearing the dust is the process of becoming

---

55 http://www.ihreiki.com/blog/article/secret_medicine/

aware of the unconscious and doing something about it. Doing something, that means accepting, healing, cleansing through various techniques: doing Reiki, using affirmations, practicing forgiveness or even visiting a psychotherapist.

In the third Reiki symbol, Hon Sha Ze Sho Nen, we can read: *nothing is separated from the true nature of Buddha*. This is one of a few correct „translations" of the symbolic meaning of this entire Reiki symbol. And this is right – based on this statement the entire ideology of Buddhism was born. No person is separated from its Buddha's nature – our true nature. But unfortunately, almost everyone is unable to see this true nature until the spiritual journey truly begins. The point of spiritual growth, in accordance with Buddhism, and in accordance with Reiki, is to relearn and rediscover our inner nature – that is good, peaceful and wise.

Our mind can be compared to the sky. There are two main states of the sky – the one during the day, and one during the night. This is where we see another meaning of the Yin and Yang symbol related to our life. Our mind has two states – the daily one and the nightly one. Between these two states we seek harmony and balance. The symbolic sky and its light is covered by dark clouds of the mind that cast shadow upon our life. These clouds are our fears, traumas, negative beliefs and opinions, unhealthy habits, toxic relationships and false limitations; but also bad memories, unhealthy life beliefs or our destructive dreams and desires. Spiritual growth is all about peaceful and gentle clearing of the clouds so that we can, once again, see our true nature, the clarity of the sky, in its Yin and Yang form.

Discovering our true nature, and discovering the clouds upon our mind, heart and soul, is a process that one way or another happens thanks to our Reiki practice, and manifests itself in many ways. Sometimes, we recall bad memories of our childhood, sometimes we become aware of negative habits that were a part of our daily life. Sometimes we try to rationalize our dreams and heal unhealthy beliefs. Sometimes we just stumble upon a book that changes a part of our life. As we face our inner darkness and our clouds of the mind, we also stumble upon our virtues – parts of our true nature – patience, the ability to accept change, peace of mind, love, ethics and so on.

It's mandatory to face the clouds of the mind if we ever wish to achieve the state of Unity and the state of happiness. We need to face the battle with ourselves, and this battle requires strength and courage – to face ourselves is the greatest life battle we ever experience. Hoff said:

> Once you face and understand your limitations, you can work with them, instead of having them work against you and get in your way, which is what they do when you ignore them, whether you realize it or not. And then you will find that, in many cases, your limitations can be your strengths.[56]

A common occurrence during Reiki practice is the return of old memories, traumas, pains, fears or beliefs that re-emerge from the subconscious mind. From the depths of the unconscious come out things we used to run away from and/or deny. What we experience here is the process of integrating the unconscious with the conscious, integrating both into a harmonious whole – the state of inner Unity. A well-known scholar of this subject, Carl Gustav Jung, said:

> Until you make the unconscious conscious, it will direct

---

56 Hoff, B., *The Tao of Pooh*, p. 48-49

your life and you will call it fate.

That which is unconscious can be called with different names: subconsciousness, the lower Self, inner child, patterns or mind matrix etc. These are some of the most popular terms.

The integration of the unconscious with the conscious is the process of self-healing. To achieve this integration over a period of years, the Reiki system provides us with the five fundamental practices. Each of these practices helps us in the process of integration, or healing that which used to be unconscious. It's worth to explore the idea of Jung's Shadow to understand it better.

Carl Gustav Jung, The Shadow and the Practice of Reiki

Jung created the concept of human Shadow – a collection of unconscious behaviors and beliefs, that from that unconscious level of our mind direct our life. Modern psychology agrees with the fact that behaviors learned and developed in the past can direct our life from the unconscious level. They direct our behavior, things we do, control our life style, or our reactions to other people and the achievement of our own goals. The unconscious can direct our way of thinking and perceiving the world, and perceiving ourselves. Our unconscious can hinder or embrace our self-worth.

Many people who are interested in spiritual growth try to seek the sources of their behaviors in the past lives. But it doesn't matter if reincarnation is a fact or no, because we do not have to seek so far away. Many obstacles that hinder our path to happiness, were developed and created in this very life, usually in our childhood, sometimes later in life. As we face these obstacles, we achieve healing. When we heal everything that was unhealthy in our life, only then we open the gates leading to something better and greater, something that leads us towards final enlightenment.

Let's get back to the idea of the Shadow – we all have our own Shadow, a collection of unconscious behaviors, beliefs, habits and thoughts. The Shadow governs our life as long as we don't acknowledge its existence and try to integrate it through self-healing: rationalization, acceptance and change.

Here are a few examples of popular effects of our Shadow:

That which irritates us in the behavior of others is usually what lies deep within ourselves and we are afraid to admit it. Sometimes that which irritates us in others is what we carry within us and are afraid of. And sometimes, it's something we envy others. All of this has been called the Shadow by Carl Gustav Jung – these are the things we do not accept in ourselves, or we consider them shameful in ourselves or against our own views of ourselves, or against the society or family.

The traumas, past experiences, all these create the Shadow. Negative way of being risen – like telling us that sex is dirty, or crying is a sign of weakness – everything that is against the human nature – all of this creates the Shadow. Every rejection, bad decision, critics made by others, this also creates the Shadow. Feeling ashamed creates Shadow. The sense of guilt creates the Shadow. Betrayal of your own soul creates the Shadow. And so on, so on. Irrational behavior is also the Shadow – behavior that used to be useful in the past, but as the time passed, this behavior is no longer useful.

This Shadow later on shapes our own life, creating it from the level of the unconscious.

Now in life, when we experience something related to our Shadow, an event of some sort, for example, we experience negative emotions: anger, fear, shame, irritation. Sometimes, these emotions might be positive and healthy, trying to save our life, or protect ourselves against real danger. But sometimes, these emotions may be irrational, as results of our Shadow, and may lead us to more problems.

Sometimes, it may happen that instead of solving the problems of our inner self, we cast these problems upon others – it's called the projection of emotions. We project these emotions onto others. This projection of emotions works like this – we are afraid of looking within ourselves to seek our own problems, so we perceive the same problems in others – what irritates us in others is what lies within us but we're afraid to look within. Our society and Western culture made us be afraid of looking within. Here's where Japanese roots of Reiki becomes important, as in Japan, looking within is very important.

So if we are afraid to look within, or if we don't know how to do this, the only way to see what lies within us is to notice it in other people – it's the only way to see our own problems. We can see the flaws of other people right away, but we can't see the same flaws within ourselves. That's what projection of the emotions is – this is the projection of our own Shadow. It's a common thing – to project our inner self onto the reality that surrounds us. Based on this common thing, the Rorschach test works, the one with ink blot that is meant to help us interpret our inner thoughts.

It's useful to learn when we actually project ourselves onto others and learn to notice that which irritates us in others, so that we can heal it within ourselves. Because quite often when we heal that thing within ourselves, it stops to irritates us in others.

These are a few examples of our own inner Shadow.

Healing with Reiki and Integrating the Shadow

The process of healing our Shadow is the process of integrating that which is unconscious into a holistic whole. An integration and acceptance of our Shadow is the process of healing. When we integrate the unconscious, even if the memories do not go away, we change our emotional reaction towards our Shadow – when we do, it stops to govern our life. This process of integration leads us to the state of inner Unity – one of the goals of Reiki practice.

One of the ways of discovering and understanding our Shadow is to observe our emotions and relations with other people, but also our emotional reactions for events and experiences. Our Shadow reflects itself in the outer world. How we perceive the world around us is our protection of our inner world onto the outer world. The Emerald Tablet says:

As above, so below. As within, so outside.

This old alchemical text shares almost Buddhist-like wisdom. The world is not what it is just because it is this way. The world is this way because we perceive it this way. We shape the world around us with our own thoughts and opinions, projecting our inner world outside. Negative experiences, failures, sad emotions, obstacles, all of this that manifest itself in our life, all of this is a sign that something negative, unpleasant – thoughts, beliefs, experiences – is being carried within our mind, heart and soul. When we become aware of these negative things and we integrate them with our conscious life, we heal ourselves. Our beliefs about the world change, and along with them, the world around us changes.

Working with our Shadow is a subject of many books and methods of therapy – to discuss the Shadow in details is not a subject of this book. But let's discuss how the practice of Reiki is related to the concept of Shadow:

1. The Gassho Kokyu Ho meditation teaches us to observe

our thoughts, instead of fighting with them. Observing our Shadow leads to integration, and fighting our Shadow only makes it stronger.

2. Self-treatment leads to integration, because they offer us spiritual energy that helps us become aware of many inner problems, thoughts and emotions. These problems often manifest themselves as energy blockages – Reiki allows us to heal these blockages.

3. The Joshin Kokyu Ho meditation gives us energy as well, but also strengthens our connection with the Earth, building a strong foundation for the following spiritual growth.

4. Working with the Reiki symbols heals and integrates each of the Diamonds, that is different aspects of our life. The symbols heal these aspects of our life. Also, working with the SHK symbol allows us to change our beliefs, traumas and heal emotions in general.

5. Working with the Five Precepts helps us discover our own Shadow and, with the help of contemplation, integrate this Shadow into our daily life, or at least become aware of the things that we can heal with general Reiki or with Symbols.

Generally, the practice of Reiki sometimes helps us become aware of the problems that we have to heal with other techniques of self-healing, but in most cases Reiki heals things by itself. It does so in more or less aware way. And sometimes, Reiki just leads us to techniques or experiences that helps us heal ourselves. The process and all its elements – everything that happens to you after Reiki class – is an individual thing. Each person experiences something different.

The only things that are common for every practitioner are the main subjects, the aspects of being human, and the process of healing itself that occurs when we practice on regular basis. It's fascinating that even when we do not know what is going on due to our practice, the process of healing continues on its own – the very simple, very basic work with Reiki makes us change our life for better.

Thanks to self-insights, the practice of Reiki clears our mind and soul of negative beliefs and behaviors, showing us our true self. When we see this true nature of our being, manifesting itself as goodness, right to live a good life, or as ethics, wisdom, love and inner peace, the further Reiki practice will strengthen and embrace these virtues, so that we can become better people for ourselves and for all living beings.

Sometimes, healing the Shadow is not a conscious act. It happens on a deep, subtle and unconscious level. As a result of working with Reiki, we experience things, for example through books, meeting new people, or experiencing emotional reactions like sudden cry or laugh, we we're not even aware of what has been healed. And yet, our life changes.

Working with Reiki develops some positive virtues within ourselves, virtues that are part of every human being, and they're natural to us. These virtues are patience, happiness, tolerance, ethics, acceptance of change, inner peace and so on.

Also, a few more words need to be said so we don't present Reiki as too difficult or harsh:

How intense this healing process of our life will be depends on our past life experiences – the more negative habits or thoughts we had in the past, the more intense Reiki healing will be. The level of practice also matters – the more we work with Reiki, the stronger the healing becomes. That's why you should guide yourself with your intuition to know how much you should practice and work with Reiki at your current moment of life. Also, remember that the amount of practice time should be increased steadily and gently. That's why, for example, we have three levels of Reiki that include more practices on each next level.

Some people will prefer a more intense healing, and others will prefer more gentle healing – and yet, every person will heal itself in a way it was meant to be. The intensity of growth and transformation is unique and individual for each person. In other words, each one of us has our own pace when it comes to Reiki.

Many people who work with Reiki experiences a gentle transformation that isn't very dramatic. And sometimes these people can't even say they experienced anything special – they life just changes for better, just like that. But I talk about the more intense and problematic experiences on the path of Reiki so that II and III degree practitioner realize these things happen and it's good to be aware of some experiences and themes on the Reiki path.

Remember – the Shadow never goes away – it is being integrated into your life. We do not trash it, we add it to a holistic whole of our being. Fighting with the Shadow, even unconsciously, is a waste of our spiritual energy. When we accept our Shadow, our energy is redirected to embrace that which is positive. This energy can freely embrace our positive view of the world.

The process of integration of the unconscious, from the Jung's perspective, goes not only to our traumas and negative beliefs, but also to our archetypes of psychological gender, accepting and integrating what we call our Anima and Animus, developing it and healing, too.

A healthy Shadow is very useful. When we have no control over that which is unconscious, it governs our life. But when our Shadow is a holistic part of us, we gain control. Our aggression can be redirected towards protection of those we love. Our stubbornness may become useful in business negotiation. Our little workaholism may become useful when something must be done quickly. Our fear can give us strength to protect ourselves. This is the path to harmony and inner Unity, in which Yin and Yang (Japan: In and Yo) works together, and not against each other.

The whole process of integration of our Shadow is a process of inner transformation – also known as Initiation. So now we need to discuss Initiation itself.

Initiation – the Path of Inner Transformation

An important element of the path of Reiki is to understand what initiation really is and how is it different from the attunement itself, or the Reiju. Understanding the difference allows us not only to establish Reiki in the human experience and tradition, but also helps us grow strength that allows us to go through the „cleansing" process after workshops successfully.

It's a common, yet false belief that Reiki initiation is a quick thing that takes no more than an hour, and it happens during Reiki class or workshop. But in reality, what happens during Reiki class is merely an attunement. This is the „Reiju", the blessing, often called a form of gift offered to you through the teacher. The teacher stands next to you and acts like a channel, as the Reiki offers you the gift of the ability to channel Reiki. But the initiation itself begins right after that and it should be understood as a path of inner transformation. The teacher cannot offer you the initiation, because the initiation is something you go through by yourself. The teacher can merely be close to you and help you understand what's going on and support you in the process.

Initiation to Reiki as a Process

Allow me to quote my own article I published on Taraka, a Polish website on spiritual traditions of the world. In the article, I discuss Reiki initiation as an inner transformation.[57]

> As it turns out, the initiation process into the Reiki practice is not the process that takes a few minutes during the classes. In reality, it's a process that may be quite painful, and it is based upon the reconstruction of the inner self so that the man or woman is ready to be a person working with spiritual energy. And just as Reiki serves as a catalyst of changes, so is the attunement merely an event that begins the entire process of initiation.
>
> (…)
>
> The initiation is an entire process of inner transformation that, with the help of Reiki, reconstructs our Inner Self. We heal this inner self this way. And this process takes more than a few minutes – it can last for weeks, even months. (...) I've been inspired to contemplate upon this matter by the length of the shamanic initiation process – something quite different from Reiki, but something that is a good base for further thoughts.
>
> (…)
>
> The initiation into Reiki is not symbolic. It's quite real, and it's a long-term inner process. It is full of obstacles, pain, and the destruction of that which is old, and that which must be destroyed in order to build your new personality. The aspect of destruction of the old in order to create the new is a common

---

57 Usarzewicz, W., *Inicjacja do Reiki jako proces, nie zaś „oświecenie instant.* [In:] Taraka.pl <http://www.taraka.pl/inicjacja_reiki_proces_nie> / English edition: http://reikipaths.com/p/attunement-reiju-and-the-process-of-initiation/124

element within many communities, and especially as a part of the rites of passage within these cultures. Like in case of a shamanism, Reiki initiation seems like a process of deconstructions the personality of a man to basic elements in order to put them back into a new, harmonious wholeness. But in case of Reiki, it's not the spirits who are responsible for deconstruction and reconstruction of the personality. It is Reiki that does this deconstruction to some degree, showing you the things that must be healed. And often, a man must reconstruct himself on his own. (...) And somewhere in the future, the goal awaits – the state of harmony and oneness. (...)

But the journey begins with the deconstruction of our personality to its basic elements, the slow process of destroying the old personality, and becoming aware of your inner darkness. And we all carry the inner darkness within us. It's a journey of realizing what is pathological within us, and what must be brought back into balance, into a state of inner harmony, and the outer harmony with our environment and Mother Nature.

(…)

The process of cleansing [after attunement] gets rid of everything that is no longer needed in our life, and this process of cleansing is part of the general initiation, a continuing process in which we must rebuild our personality – get rid of something old, and introduce something new to our life.

(…)

This initiation is what prepares the person to be a Reiki practitioner who will help others. The initiation is meant to destroy that which is destructive and dangerous in our life, that which destroys our inner balance and harmony between the physical, emotional and spiritual realm, and further on, between the individual person and the society and the Nature that surrounds it.

(...)

Due to the process of initiation, we come to realize the toxic relationship we may have. We break old relationship in order to create a new, better one. We drop old spiritual practices that never gave us anything so we can reach new practices with greater benefits. We drop old eating habits to introduce more healthy diet in our life. Those are just examples of the things we may experience. Some of these life changes is subtle and small, that we may not realize that the change is occurring. Other changes are big and loud, and they may scare those around us who must get used to our new selves. And this process continues as long as it is needed. For some people, the changes may be small and subtle, even invisible. To other people, the changes may be huge and loud, even dramatic.

Malidoma Some says this about the shamanic initiation:

> The wounds made to you are a casing for the gold that you carry deep inside you. In order to find the gold, you must break through the wounds. In order to get to the real treasure that will make you feel proud of yourself, we must experience pain first. That is what initiation is about.[58]
>
> *- Dagar's Shaman Malidoma Some (source: Lubke, G., von. Dawna madrosc na nowe czasy. Rozmowy z uzdrawiaczami i szamanami XXI wieku. Warszawa 2009, page 194. Original title: Altes Wissen fur eine neue Zeit. Gesprache mit Heilern und Schamanen des 21. Jahrhunderts.)*

---

58 Lubke, G. von. *Dawna mądrość na nowe czasy*, p. 194.

(...)

And often all of this is a hard work, and a painful experience. Because we must face the greatest foe – ourselves. We must stand in front of a mirror and look on something that looks like a battlefield full of wreckage, caused by the healing energy. Because often, in order to begin healing, we must destroy the old structures of our life.

(...)

When the old structures are gone, we receive a chance to replace them with new structures.

(...)

It's because that which comes to light thanks to Reiki has to be healed. Otherwise, with greater strength it will control our life. This will lead only to more chaos and problems.

(...)

The initiation into Reiki should be understood as a long, continuing process and a journey of the person, a quest for... what? Understanding, Buddha's nature, enlightenment, our Self. The initiation into Reiki should be understood as the process of rebuilding the personality and psyche of the man, along with the dreams, virtues and values. The goal of this is to make the person a good, valuable practitioner, but also to make the person capable of achieving spiritual harmony – both the inner one, and the outer one, the harmony with the world.

Initiation to Reiki is a path of inner transformation, and the attunement during classes is merely a point to start the journey of change that will begin right away.

A well-known scholar of cultures and primal rites, Robert L. Moore, defines three main stages in an archetypal initiation:

destruction, grieve and regeneration (rebirth), or in other words: crisis, grieve and reintegration.[59] Let's give an example, when we break up with someone, we first experience pain because the process of destruction takes place. After ending a relationship, we have to face grieve. But then, we should experience regeneration and rebirth. The old structures must be destroyed and closed in the past (we have to accept the lost or change), and only then we can make changes for better in our life. Only by ending the past stages of our life we can begin a new stage.

Once again I recall the story from the beginning of this book – in order to pour the tea, we need to empty the cup first from the previous drink. In the Reiki initiation, the process of destruction manifests itself on many levels: old beliefs are being destroyed, unhealthy diet is destroyed, laziness is destroyed, but also our destructive habits, interests, toxic relationships or fears are destroyed.

The example I gave you earlier was about love relationship, but it can very well be about puberty or changing the job. We all experience different initiations in life, even when we do not think of these experiences as initiations. But they are. A deeper form of these processes is a spiritual initiation, for example an initiation into Reiki, or shamanic initiation. Here, as well, in a spiritual context, we observe destruction of the old structures, the time of healing (grieve) and the process of integration.

An important part of the initiation to discuss is the second part – the time of grieve and healing. Otherwise, without his part, reintegration and rebirth will never occur. During this stage of transformation, we need to work with ourselves: do Reiki, contemplate, change our beliefs, habits, lifestyle, relationships – and we do this through healing techniques, reading or trusting the

---

59 Havlick, M. J., Jr [ed.], *The Archetype of Initiation*, p. 20-21.

experiences we have. The integration must be complete – if in your heart you do not belief you're ready for another level of Reiki, don't do it. The initiation is a journey into our inner self so that we can heal things we find there. This is also a process in which we give up the life stability and we take the journey of many dangers and painful experiences. What we learn from these experiences defines if we complete the initiation successfully or not.

The Aspects of Successful Initiation

Moore tells us about three important aspects of successful initiation. It's the (1) will to go with the process, (2) proper space and (3) taking new actions.[60] First we need to decide if we truly want to go with the process. We must become submissive, we must allow others to direct us so that the process of initiation begins, even if we are aware of the fact it won't be pleasant. In case of Reiki, we become „submissive" to the teacher (we're talking about archetypal submission – not sexual or financial or any other type of negative submission). We learn to trust the teacher, we sit and allow him or her to perform attunement. Then, the initiation itself starts and we become submissive to Reiki itself and everything that Reiki wish to throw at us, like destruction of the old and grieve. To pass this stage, we need safety, some kind of sacred space. Sometimes, this requires the person to find shelter within its own mind, hide from the world – the people, family, friends, but also from the old habits.

The practitioner of Reiki cuts the ties with the world for some time and seek peace, a place for contemplation. In the old days, people used to go into the wild to seek visions (experience vision quests). Today, the practitioner can go on vacation, or just set an hour per day for his own privacy so that no one can disturb him or

---

60 Ibidem, p. 61-69.

her. This is how we create our own sacred space in which we are safe with everything that requires healing. This sacred space can be constructed. It can be peace, quiet and a cup of good tea as symbols of personal sacredness; or incenses, candles and meditation pose that defines the space in which the practitioner faces himself or herself.

Thus, you should make sure that after attending Reiki class you will be able to have some privacy for yourself. It can be half an hour of peace and quiet for your self-treatment, or it can be a retreat to a mountain cabin.

With the work in sacred space, the practitioner of Reiki must move to the third stage of initiation – taking action and defining new rules. This is where personal strength manifests: we may need to break old relationships, take new actions, give up old habits, accept new beliefs. This is where theory and contemplation shifts into real life action. This is where a human being – the practitioner of Reiki – gets out from the sacred space into the world, and returns to the people, changed. And this is where something important happens.

You see, there are three aspects of successful initiation as it has been said earlier: your current state of consciousness that needs to be changed is one thing. As we start the initiation process, we begin the inner transformation. This is where destruction of old structures begins. Then we enter the second sage, that is the stage of limbo, being frozen in stasis, being lost – this is where we find ourselves anew in the sacred space. We want to be transformed because we realize we cannot live with the old structures any more. And when we find ourselves anew, we begin the process of integration. And as we integrate ourselves into a whole again, the final element of initiation occurs, one that is a signal the initiation has been completed: it's the return to normal.[61]

A Reiki practitioner can notice this at some point – after long and hard work with our own mind, soul and heart, full of surprises, shifts, fireworks and experiences, the practitioner goes back to normal. Suddenly, everything seems normal again – there are no more surprises. Normal life happens just like that with all its pains, happiness, good and evil, shopping and cooking for the family. This return to normal, to everything that is ordinary, is a signal that the initiation is completed. We're different now, we were transformed, we completed our inner transformation. As long as we can't find stability in our life, as long as things do not seem normal, and we experience a lot of spiritual stuff, it is a signal that our initiation is not yet completed, or what's worse, we may be stuck in the moment, stuck in a belief that we have completed the initiation – while in reality, we didn't.

We recognize the completion of initiation process by recognizing we live a normal life once again. The old Zen saying goes like this: before enlightenment, mountains were mountains. During enlightenment, mountains were no longer mountains. After enlightenment, mountains were mountains again. After experiencing the normal again, you learn and recognize you've finished that particular stage of your Reiki journey.

Polishing the Diamonds

After completing your first degree class of Reiki, you should wait for at least six months before you take the second degree class. And after second degree, you should wait at least one to two years before taking the third degree. In traditional Usui Shiki Ryoho, a student was accepted to the next level only after the teacher decided the student was ready. Years could have passed

---

61 Ibidem, p. 78-80.

before the person was ready to take the next step.

One thing you can be sure of – every school of spiritual thought says this that every problem in your life should be considered a spiritual experience, a point in which we can make change in our life. If we get stuck, if we stop acting and we will flow with the river of suffering, then we will experience fall. But if we can see opportunities in our painful experiences, if we consider these experiences as life lessons that shape our character and personality, then we will embrace our soul, and the painful experiences will be a base to start a better life.

It is said that

A Smooth Sea Never Made a Skillful Sailor.

In the same way, a life without problems will not form a strong personality. The difference between a strong and weak person is that the weak person kneels before his problems, and the strong person uses the problem to grow. Even the historic Buddha, Sidharta Gautama, experienced both abundance as a prince and poverty as a seeker of truth. In the end, by collecting his experiences together, he discovered the middle path, that later on changed into the ideology of Buddhism.

A popular metaphor says that a man is an unpolished diamond, and the tools that polish him, that allow him to shine and glow, are „brutal" and „aggressive". These painful experiences: becoming aware of our fears, traumas, beliefs, and all these crisis experiences on the path of spiritual growth, all of this is the process of polishing the Three Diamonds that create the whole of human existence.

In similar way, a Waka poem goes:[62]

---

62 Complete list of Waka poems can be found in "The Spirit of Reiki" by Rand,

95 – Mine
If there were
A mountain of gold, radiating
How can you
See the light
Without opening[63]

We must pierce through the pain and suffering (old structures) that grew upon us to see the glow radiating from our soul.

***

To summarize, healing the physical illness through Reiki is a result of working with both that which is physical and that which is spiritual. That which is spiritual is represented by the Earth Diamond, associated with the Hara. That which is mental and emotional is represented by the Heaven Diamond, associated with the head. And the spiritual integration of both is represented by the Diamond of Heart. Each of the Reiki symbols is associated with one of the Three Diamonds, but also the Reiki techniques are associated with these Diamonds. Joshin Kokyu Ho is focused on the Hara. Mental treatment, Seiheki Chiryo, is focused on the head. Gassho and Five Precepts helps us integrate the Three Diamonds.

Becoming aware of the negative aspects of the unconscious helps us heal bad memories, helps us repair relationship, change our diet and habits, but also helps us find preferred directions on the spiritual path. These are the effects of integration.

And the integration of the unconscious leads us to uniting the

Petter and Lubeck.

63 Lubeck, Petter, Rand, *The Spirit of Reiki*, p. 294

light and darkness (Shadow) within us – that which is Yin and that which is Yang – into a harmonious whole. Thanks to this, we achieve the state of Unity with ourselves and with the world around us. This state of Unity is full of inner peace, happiness, spiritual strength, ethics, tolerance, compassion, love and wisdom.

As a result of all of this, our physical health gets better and our happiness becomes greater. And all of this is a result of working with the Five Elements of Reiki.

Five Elements of Reiki

In order to integrate Three Diamonds together, and to integrate the unconscious into conscious and discover our true nature full of ethics, goodness, happiness and inner peace, the path of Reiki is made of Five Elements. The practice of these elements changes our life for better, and we begin to experience the state of Unity with ourselves and the world around us.

But, we should not mistake the Five Elements with the Five Goals; the Five Goals being taught in Japanese organization Usui Reiki Ryoho Gakkai. These goals, though, are worth to mention, as the knowledge of the Five Goals can support our practice further by directing us to things we should look for on the path of Reiki.

The Five Goals of Reiki practice that should be achieved through daily work, according to Gakkai, are:[64]

1. **Tai-ken** – a healthy body, a temple of human being that

64 Petter, F.A., *This is Reiki*, p. 251.

must be taken care of, especially because, according to Buddhist teachings, only a healthy body can survive the moment of enlightenment. The body is strengthen by healthy diet or meditation.

2. **En-Bi** – it's a state in which we notice beauty, wisdom and glory in every living being, and in everything that exists, as well. When we are able to see this in everything that is, our life becomes better.
3. **Kokoro-Makoto** – a state in which unity of mind and heart is achieved through being honest with oneself.
4. **Sai-Chikara** – it's a talent and personal power. When you live your life and you utilize all your talents, then you gain great power and inner strength. Then, life stops to scare you, because things happen to you with great ease.
5. **Tsutome-Do** – a personal duty for personal growth.

As you progress with your daily practice of Reiki, you should intend for these goals to be achieved. Our practice is based on the Five Elements. These Five Elements are a foundation for our practice. We can compare them to proper foundation of the building that allows the structure to stand for generations; or to big roots of a great and healthy tree, that won't fall even when stroke with powerful winds. Practices, such as Yoga or Qigong, survived for so long because they had strong foundation, upon which a strong, steady spiritual practice could have been built. The practice of Reiki, also, can survive and develop only when the foundation of the Five Elements is kept close to your heart.

The Roots and Basics for the Practice of Reiki

Every spiritual practice requires strong roots, or stable foundation, upon which the practice will be build. My teacher,

Arkadiusz Lisiecki, used to remind me all the time that the true spiritual growth starts only after third degree of Reiki; the years of Shoden and Okuden practice that precede it are merely a process of building the foundation for the real spiritual practice.

The foundation (the basics for the practice) can be categorized as theoretical and cultural, and as practical. The theoretical-cultural basics were described in this book already. We recognize them in knowledge and culture of Japan. These are the basics that make Reiki practice so successful. In addition to that, we have the knowledge of practical basics and foundation – the Five Elements – which are practices, techniques and exercises.

For some people the Five Elements are an integral part of Reiki teachings. Meaning, the term is important and is closely related to the roots of the Reiki practice, even if the term itself is modern. For other people, Five Elements are merely a modern concept popularized by Bronwen and Frans Stienes, who created the term of „Five Elements".

Thus, it must be pointed out that the concept of Five Elements is not a tradition passed from generation to generation, but a modern recreation of old traditional Reiki ideas, as based on available sources. Even so, this concept, when put to practice, offers us real results on our path of spiritual growth.

The concept is simple – the Five Elements is a minimum amount of knowledge and techniques that must be learned by a Reiki practitioner in order to get the best results in Reiki practice. **Five Elements of Reiki are an important part of the path of Three Diamonds.** Here are the elements:

1. Attunement, that is Reiju.
2. Integration of the Five Precepts (Gokai) into your daily life.

3. Breathing techniques and meditations, such as Kenyoku Ho or Joshin Kokyu Ho.
4. Four Symbols of Reiki and their mantras.
5. Healing through touch – treatments and self-treatments.

All of these elements will be described on the following pages as integral elements of Reiki system. Regular practice of these elements will result in strong and stable spiritual effects. But, when I teach Reiki, I say that the absolute basics of Reiki is the practice of self-treatments that are enough to get results. I do not deny this fact – every person that has completed Shoden class should remember that if you wish to experience positive results of Reiki, do self-treatment and that will be enough.

What to Practice, How to Practice

Indeed, self-treatment is an absolute basic for most practitioners. But in the end, it's Reiki that defines and decides what you will practice and how intense practice it will be. Reiki does this by guiding you on your individual path of spiritual growth; by inspiring and showing new things, sometimes not even related to Reiki itself. In result, practitioners can be categorized into two main types: ordinary Joe Doe that will practice self-treatment and it will be enough for him, because his speed of spiritual growth is perfect for him. The second type will be the full-time practitioners of Reiki. For them, Reiki may become the only spiritual path to practice. It's for them, for this second type of people, why the concept of Three Diamonds and Five Elements becomes important, because these people will notice a value in these teachings.

Of course, there's always the third type, the middle path, in which someone may seek harmony between full-time Reiki practitioner and ordinary Joe Doe approach.

Further, all Five Elements can be practiced equally – then, our practice is intense but also takes a lot of time. Yet for many people, I have good news – we can practice individual Elements, for example choose one or two Elements to work with.

On one hand, it's a great thing for a Western person with limited time, but on the other hand, there's a deeper truth in this. For example, visual people will prefer to work with symbols themselves, for example through visualization. Those who prefer sound will prefer to chant the symbols, for example. People who prefer to meditate will benefit more from Gassho or Joshin Kokyu Ho meditations. And everyone who won't easily fall asleep in relaxed state will benefit from self-treatments and Reiju blessings.

Dalailama said the following words about general practice of Buddhism:

> (...) When dying, the best practitioner is happy to change his body for a better one to practice Dharma. A practitioner who practice from time to time is ready for death. And the practitioner who practices the least has no regrets.[65]

In the same manner, even the smallest practice of Reiki will bring positive results if it's an honest and true practice. Remember about the strength of Kaji – if you have pure and honest intentions in your heart and mind, and you wish to heal yourself and become a better person, then even the shortest and smallest practice will offer us that which we need the most.

Of course, it's not about making things too easy – don't limit yourself to one of the Elements only because it's easier. If time and

---

65 His Holiness Dalailama, *Przebudzenie umysłu, rozświetlanie serca*, p. 69. (author's translation)

honesty of your intentions allows you to do so, then practice as much as possible. Do not limit yourself because of laziness, yet practice that which resonates with you the most, whether it's self-treatment, symbols or chanting etc.

The Need for Intense Practice

In the end, though, only an intense practice of all Five Elements will offer you the best results possible. For example, every time you experience Reiju (or western attunement), our capability of channeling Reiki energy increases, which allows us to face and heal bigger and bigger Shadows we may have in our heart and mind. Regular self-treatment recharges our spiritual batteries and heal that which comes out from the unconscious during daily practice. Working with the four symbols of Reiki and their jumons brings things out from the unconscious as well. Gassho meditation helps us heal our monkey mind and chaotic thoughts by bringing peace to our thoughts. Joshin Kokyu Ho develop the strength of our mind and body and our capabilities of working with Reiki energy. Working with the Five Precepts (Gokai) brings out more Shadows from the unconscious, and allows us to consciously face our unhealthy beliefs or behaviors, also developing our inner ethics. And all of this makes it easier for us to face our fears, problems and daily challenges of life.

Taking care of practice of Five Elements is very important, especially for people to decide to seriously walk the path of Reiki as a spiritual practice through all three degrees and then facing the dangers of the Shinpiden, not to mention the intention to teach Reiki to other people. On one hand, the practice of Five Elements makes the practitioner heal enough things to safely face the third degree, thus acting as a good and ethical Reiki teacher becomes possible for this person. On the other hand, knowing the Five

Elements helps the teacher to pass them further to his or hers own students, keeping the lineage of useful knowledge intact so that other people can benefit from it, as well.

That's why all the Five Elements are going to be discussed in this book in as many details as possible so that you can understand the Elements as best as possible.

I will discuss the Reiju and its meaning; four symbols and their jumons along with mandatory information regarding both. I will describe the practice of traditional techniques, mainly the Gassho meditation and Joshin Kokyu Ho, along with detailed descriptions on their effects upon spiritual growth of the practitioner. Remember that regular and honest practice of the Five Elements will lead you to integrate the Three Diamonds in your heart, thus leading to the state of harmony and Unity with yourself and with the world around you. As this integration progresses, the daily life becomes better and better.

Reiju, or the Blessing

While it's a common belief that Reiki is something that is received as a gift, it's a bit far from the truth. Reiki is not a mystical symbol engraved into the "aura", and it is not a secret spell that allows us to work with energy. In reality, Reiki is a spiritual force, a force that brings harmony back. Access to this force is a part of human nature – to be able to work with Reiki is part of our Buddha's nature. The attunement to Reiki, also known as Reiju, can be compared to a key – with this key, the teacher opens the door to something that was hidden and dormant within us – yet still present.

Using this key awakens our inner ability to work with Reiki energy. Under the term "Reiju" at least two things can be found. First, a traditional blessing; second, a western attunement. Both these terms represent a useful and important practice of Reiju. Let's discuss them now.

Traditional seiza.

Tradition states that Reiju is understood as a physical and energetic ritual, in which the student sits in traditional seiza sit, or on a chair, and the teacher performs an energetic act around the student. This energetic process is just a form of channeling Reiki energy which is known to teachers. The physical part of this process is a set of physical gestures and movements such as placing hands in Gassho or chanting Reiki symbols. The energetic part is controlled by teacher's intention, and the physical gestures are merely to strengthen these intentions.

While receiving the Reiju, the student practices Joshin Kokyu Ho meditation. The goal of this is to create a sacred space, in which the student will draw the spiritual energy into himself, and his physical spiritual and physical body will remember the process so that in the future, the student can draw Reiki energy on his own, without the need for teacher.[66]

It's worth to mention that in the western attunements the student does not „draw" anything in and practice nothing but breathes and relax during the attunement. Also, it's important not to change the western attunement, which is successful enough, just to make it look more traditional. Stiene says that Mikao Usui used to practice Reiju without physical contact nor gestures – the gestures were added later on, perhaps during Hayashi time, in order to strengthen the intentions of the Reiju blessing. Later on, symbols were introduced and in results, modern attunement process was created. But, since we do not have proper sources on the matter, we cannot say that Usui didn't teach classic, „western" form of attunements. Whether he did so or not, remains a mystery. Still, it's a fact that modern western form of attunements works just as good as the traditional practice.

In the west, we practice small number of attunements that are merely a good minimum for successful practice. They allow us to work with Reiki through our entire life. That said, traditional Reiju was considered a form of spiritual blessing and the student used to receive it more or less once a week, or at least every time the student met with the teacher. Such Reiju blessing offered the student additional strength on the spiritual path, speeding up the growth of the student. Of course, that doesn't mean Reiju was faster. On the contrary, Reiju was offered only when the teacher could see real progress in the student's life. And only because of this progress, a result of daily and honest Reiki practice, the Reiju blessing had sense and worth.

In Reiju itself we do not see any kind of abilities being passed

---

66 Stiene, B., Stiene F., *Japanese Art of Reiki*, p. 133-4.

onto a student – Reiju merely creates a space, in which a human being recalls the natural ability to work with Reiki. It's a process of reconnecting with the Source, and rediscovering the state of Unity with our inner Buddha's nature. This way, a person regains the natural ability to work with Reiki – everything else, such as hand positions or breathing techniques, are add-ons that makes the natural ability into a unified system.

Chris Marsh, a well-respected Reiki scholar, said that Reiju[67] is being passed in a state of pure consciousness and awareness with great compassion, with no strings attached, without desire for specific results of this process.[68]

Reiju has at least three levels:

1. The level of connection – the essence of practice, in which the student re-learns the existence of Reiki and the ability to work with this energy.
2. The level of cleansing – in which Reiki energy heals every energetic area of the body, clearing it and increasing the natural ability to channel this healing, spiritual energy.
3. The physical level – in which, through physical gestures, the teacher connects with the student on an energetic level, so that Reiju can be performed.

In a way, to receive Reiju or western form of attunement is to admit in front of the world that we are ready to begin our own, individual spiritual path.

Reiju can be experienced multiple times – every time we may

---

67 It's possible that Reiju tradition originates from Tendai teachings and is similar to "Go Shimbo" practice, which is known as Dharma for the Protection of the Body.

68 Ibidem, p. 134.

experience something different. But whether Reiju will or will not have any results for us, depends only on our own commitment for spiritual practice.

To translate it for our western concepts, you can receive the attunement only once and Reiki will remain with you for the rest of your life. In traditional Japanese Reiki you could experience Reiki many times. The teacher was offering it when he felt the student was ready. Each next Reiju increased the ability to work with Reiki and allowed the student to heal more things and pursuit harmony further. In western Reiki, all of this w as enclosed in one-time attunement. That said, nothing stops you from experiencing the western attunement multiple times. You can also find a teacher that offers traditional Reiju. But to master traditional Reiju is not possible through reading books. It is a result of longer, honest and difficult work with the fourth symbol of Reiki, the DKM – thus, finding the right teacher may be a challenge.

Reiju Tips for Student

When you head for Reiki class, you may think that you just need to hear the teacher out, sit down on a chair and let the teacher do his job. But, an important aspect of attunement is the student's approach, and it's important on to levels.

First, for successful Reiju, the student must trust the teacher. The more we trust our teacher, the better the Reiki flow is. Of course, the teacher must deserve to be trusted. He should be good, ethical, friendly. That's why it's so important to find the right teacher, one that we „feel” intuitively. It's the first state of successful attunement. But it's still not enough. You must also awake your true intention of self-healing and personal growth, because only honest intentions will open us for the flow of Reiki that will guide us further. When you go to learn Reiki, you need to actually want to change your life for better, and mainly take responsibility for your own healing and your own life instead of casting this responsibility onto others.

Also, remember that when the student practice a lot, then Reiki flows better, thus any next Reiju gives better results. On the other hand, the honesty and experience of the teacher also influences the quality of the Reiju. Thus, when the student and teacher both continue to grow and heal themselves, then the Reiju experience between them offers even better results.

Reiju Tips for the Teacher

Often, the teacher thinks that all he has to do is to make a few gestures above the student and Reiki will do the rest. But the successfulness of Reiju depends a lot on the spiritual growth level of the teacher. That is why the role of the teacher should be taken only by those practitioners who honestly devoted themselves to the practice of Reiki and spiritual growth, so that they won't become slaves of money or fame.

The more Reiki you practice as a Shinpiden practitioner and the more Shadows you heal, the clearer your hearts become, your intentions become more honest, and your awareness of your Buddha's nature increases. The closer to the state of Unity you are, the better Reiki practitioner you become, and that results in your ability to offer even better Reiju. That's why the practice of Five Elements is mandatory for you if you wish to become a Reiki teacher one day.

In Reiju itself, you need to approach the student with pure intentions and with Buddhist compassion and the idea of Kaji in your heart. Reiju is not just a ritual full of gestures, but mainly a state of mind of the teacher. A state of goodness in which the teacher channels pure Reiki. In order for the teacher to do so, to offer successful Reiju or western attunement, an intense practice with the fourth symbol, DKM, is also very important.

Before each Reiju (attunement), the teacher should perform the following practice.

1. Become aware of your goal, that is to offer pure and honest Reiju to the student. Relax your physical body, your mind and focus on your Hara, then place your hands in Gassho.
2. Perform Kenyoku Ho to cleanse yourself spiritually, then place both your hands on your Hara.
3. Focus on the DKM symbol, visualize it in your Hara and active it by saying its name three times. You may chant the symbol aloud. Then, keep your focus on the Hara and on the symbol itself until you feel strong connection with the symbol and the Reiki itself.
4. Place your hands in Gassho and perform the Reiju/attunement.

This is the technique worth of practicing before each attunement or Reiju.

Furthermore, it's useful to become familiar with the Kanji for Reiju itself. *Rei* is traditionally understood as rain. On one hand we talk here about a spiritual practitioner (a shaman) who asks the Heaven for the rain, and the rain falls down – it's a traditional meaning of the *Rei* ideogram. But more than that, in its spiritual meaning, the rain just falls down – it does not judge the things it falls upon. It falls down upon earth, plants, trees and never judge, just falls down – and that which the rain falls upon uses the rain for its own purposes. In the same way, the Reiki teacher and the student should remember all of this. The teacher should allow

Reiki to flow, and the student should just let it go and receive Reiki. Without judging or deciding how the energy should flow or what should it give.

The *Ju* means „to receive" - here's the secret of receiving the Reiju that says: to receive, you must first let go. You need to let go of all your intentions – why you need Reiki, why you choose Reiki, how does it work, how to feel it, what may happen afterwards and so on. The mind should be clear and open. Let Reiki flow without interruption.[69] Both the student and the teacher should keep this in mind.

Going Back to the Source through Reiju

Frans and Bronwen Stiene explain that Reiki is within every one of us, because in reality, Reiki is in everything that lives, in every living being. It fills the entire Universe. Up to this day, a few notes survived that were written down by students of Mikao Usui. Sometimes, Usui used to offer individual teachings to students who were deeply interested in the art of Reiki.

This is what the students wrote down about Reiki – we may believe that these are the beliefs of Usui himself.[70]

> "Everything in the Universe possesses Reiki without any exception."

> "We humans hold the Great Reiki that fills the Great Universe. The higher we raise the vibration of our own being, the stronger the Reiki we have inside will be."

---

69 See: http://www.ihreiki.com/blog/article/the_secret_of_reiju

70 Rand, W. L., *Interview With Hiroshi Doi Sensei*. [IN:] Reiki News Magazine, Spring 2014, no 1. Vision Publications.

"The Natural Law of the Great Universe and each human spirit as a small universe must be constantly united and exists as One."

"The Universe exists in me, and I exist in the Universe."

"Komyo exists in me and I exist in Komyo[71]."

"Everything in the universe is produced and developed by the magnificent Reiki that fills the Great Universe. Humans are a microcosm that takes the Great Spirit from macrocosm; everyone hold a part of this Great Reiki in his body. Therefore, we must always try to cultivate spirituality so that we can receive as much Great Reiki of the Universe as possible."

"The training according to the Natural Law of this whole world develops human spirituality. When you are convinced of this Truth, your committed training brings about the unification with the Universe. The words you speak and the actions you take become one with the Universe and they effortlessly work as the absolute limitlessness. This is the true nature of being human."

We may say that Reiki is a part of Buddha's nature in every person. Reiki is a path leading to Unity with everything that exists; and as a result, leading to reaching the state of Buddha. Entering the path of Reiki is available to us through Reiju, reminding us that the Buddha's nature is within us already. Reiju is the first step in going back to the Source.

---

71 Komyo – the light of enlightenment, like in the symbol "Dai Ko Myo"

Gassho

Gassho mudra is a traditional element of Reiki practice, present all the time in the practice. Ignored by some modern practitioners for unknown reasons, it's a mudra of palms put together like for a prayer. It's a mudra originating in the tradition of Buddhism. Gassho has real, positive effects when it comes to self-healing and spiritual growth.

Gassho is present in many Reiki practices, such as Gassho meditation. With this mudra we open ourselves to the flow of Reiki, and we thank for this spiritual force after practice is done. With this mudra we open all Reiki meditations, and Gassho is present during attunements (Reiju) themselves, when the teacher asks the student to put palms together in front of the student's heart, and energy is channeled into these hands.

The word „Gassho" literally means „to put palms together", but in spiritual understanding the symbolic meaning is closer to the popular word „namaste"[72] and it can be understood as:

„I recognize the Buddha in You."

By placing our hands in Gassho, we recognize a living, spiritual being in another person with all this person's characteristics; we stand as equals with this person, manifesting the Buddhist ideal of Compassion for all living beings.[73] Gassho also points a proper focus – we not only show respect to the practice we're beginning, but we also focus our mind and direct it towards concentrations and peace.

What is important is that hands put together in front of the heart

---

72 We translate "namaste" as "The spirit within me recognizes the spirit within you."

73 Stiene, B., Stiene, F., *The Reiki Sourcebook*, p. 150-151.

positively affect the second dantien (known in western pop-culture as the Heart Chakra). In the traditions of the East, the heart was a symbol of higher emotions and thoughts: goodness, compassion, wisdom and pure love. These higher emotions and feelings cannot be learned from books. They awake on their own, as we progress on the path of spiritual growth and self-healing. To practice Gassho, either in meditation or during daily Reiki work, means to clear our heart out of all pain, lower emotions and feelings, and to open our path to awake the higher feelings. Feelings that, when manifested in the real world, allows us to act for the highest good of all living beings.

Thus, you should not give up this mudra. On the contrary, you should use it as often as possible during regular Reiki practice, accepting that it is an important element of general Usui Shiki Ryoho Reiki.

Reiju, Western Practice and Modern Civilization

Now that we understand the deeper aspect of Reiju, we can decide whether we wish to experience it only once or multiple times. Reiju is repeated on all degrees in the Western version of the practice. But if we wish, we can repeat these attunements many times, whenever we feel in our heart that we're ready and that it will be beneficial to us. To make the decision, you should listen to your heart and intuition.

But it must be remembered that no matter for the traditional meaning of the Reiju, a typical „western" attunement to the first degree (Shoden) is truly enough to work with Reiki energy for the rest of person's life. Multiple Reiju is not mandatory. Regular practice of Five Elements will give results positive enough when approached with honest intentions.

Five Reiki Precepts and the Secret of Happiness

Another important aspect of Reiki practice is the work with Five Precepts, known also under their Japanese term, *Gokai*. Working with this Elements of Reiki is often neglected by practitioners, which is a mistake.

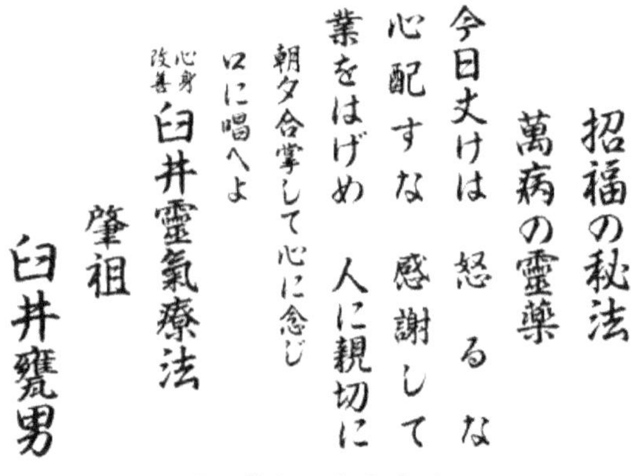

Traditional Gokai.

In reality, the Five Precepts are an integral part of Reiki system. More than that, their a true foundation for the practice. The Precepts direct us for the essence of the practice, the state of Unity which we achieve only due to regular practice. This state can be characterized as full of inner peace and happiness, gratitude and great compassion to all living beings. Frans and Bronwen Stiene points out that Reiki Precepts are the actual teachings of Usui, not just an add on. In reality, it seems that four other Elements like

Reiju, meditations etc, are the actual add-ons to the foundation of the Precepts.[74]

The Precepts themselves evolved along with the rest of the Usui's teachings. Based on available sources, we may say that the Precepts are a mixture of Meiji's Waka poems and old Buddhist ethical teachings that were part of the Shugendo practice. In some way, the Precepts are also related to the Noble Eightfold Path. The Noble Eightfold Path says that a Buddhist practitioner should focus on: right view, right intention, right speech, right action, right livelihood, right effort, right mindfulness, right concentration (meditation).[75] The word „right" means a particular ethical stance, ethical and right from the perspective of Buddhism. Living by these ethical guidelines results in achieving inner and outer peace – something similar can be achieved through integration of the Gokai into our daily life.

Deeper Understanding of the Gokai

Below you can see the Gokai in their original version and in English version – this is what the practitioner works with.[76]

---

74 Stiene, B., Stiene F., *Japanese Art of Reiki*, p. 68

75 See: http://www.accesstoinsight.org/lib/authors/bodhi/waytoend.html

76 See: Usarzewicz, W., *Droga Reiki.*

Original Version	**English version**[77]
Shoufuku no hihoo	*The secret of inviting happiness*
Manbyo no ley-yaku	*through many blessings*
Kyo dake wa	*The spiritual medicine for all*
Okoru-na	*illness*
Shimpai suna	*For today only:*
Kansha shite	*Do not anger*
Goo hage me	*Do not worry*
Hito ni shinsetsu ni	*Be humble*
Asa yuu gassho shite, koko-ro ni	*Be honest in your work*
nenji, kuchi ni tanaeyo	*Be compassionate to yourself and*
Shin shin kaizen, Usui Reiki	*others*
Ryoho	*Do gassho every morning and*
Chosso Usui Mikao	*evening*
	Keep in your mind and recite
	Improve your mind and body
	Usui Reiki Ryoho Founder Usui
	Mikao

When we known the Precepts, we can dig deeper in their spiritual meaning and role in the practice of Reiki. Most sources offers only the middle part of the Gokai to these source's readers that starts with „For today only...", and ending with the Precept related to compassion. But Gokai is more than that – it's the introduction and the final phrases, too.

The introduction to Gokai goes:

> The secret of inviting happiness through many blessings.
> The spiritual medicine for all illness.

---

77 Chris Marsh translation.

According to Frans Stiene, the term „medicine" should be understood as practices that helps us heal our inner self.[78] Those are practices of spiritual growth and healing present in the system of Reiki. And what's the „Secret"? These are the things that are realized through the practice of the Precepts (become conscious). All the things that are present within us and require healing are the secrets. They must be healed, so that, in result, positive manifestation of the Precepts becomes possible in our life. Until things become conscious, they remain a secret, a mystery, and esoteric - kept within.

The blessings, on the other hand, are all the things that manifest in our life as results of regular practice. We experience them when we integrate the Gokai into our daily life through regular and honest practice of other four Elements of Reiki. These blessings flow onto the practitioner himself first, then onto his close surroundings, and then, due to popularization of Reiki, onto the entire local community, nation, and the entire world.

The words that end the Precepts goes:

> Do Gassho every morning and evening. Keep in your mind and recite.

This part points out the way the Gokai should be worked with in the basic practice. Many people forget the importance of the Gassho and reciting the Gokai from their heart. The Precepts become a neglected way too often, and sometimes when they're recited, they're merely blindly repeated. But this phrase that ends the Gokai is an instruction of basic practice. You just need to open your heart and recite the Precepts honestly, with your hands placed in Gassho. Do this every morning and every evening. Each day, try

---

78 See: http://www.ihreiki.com/blog/article/secret_medicine/

to live by the guidelines, try to follow the ethical path represented by the Gokai. This ending phrase is also a way the practitioner learns that the Precepts are important, and they're an integral element of Reiki practice. They should not be neglected.

Further, we read:

(…) Improve your mind and body.

The body and the mind – that which is earthly and daily, and that which is emotional and spiritual – the two out of three Diamonds. Healing and growth of these Diamonds leads to happiness in life, and then creates the Third Diamond, the Diamond of the Heart. This final diamond's integration creates the whole human being, and introduces the state of Unity, and realization of Buddha's nature.

The Precepts may seem like not much because of their simplicity, but don't be mislead. A Reiki practitioner should not neglect the Precepts – regular practice of the Gokai makes the Precepts actually manifest in life.

Let's read how the Usui Reiki Ryoho Gakkai speaks of the Precepts.[79] These are another way of interpreting the Gokai, one that adds more understanding and knowledge.

1. **Okoru-na** – in the first precept, „don't get angry", the point is not to suppress anger, but to learn how to control it, observe it and learn from it. It's also about being honest towards others: speaking your mind, embracing your true feelings.
2. **Shinpai suna** - „don't worry", because regular practice of Reiki deals with worries for you.

---

79 Petter, F.A., *This is Reiki*, p. 252.

3. **Kansha shite** - „show Compassion", but also, truly embrace it in your own heart. Learn to live in a state of Compassion all the time.
4. **Goo hage me** - „work on yourself", but don't force yourself to anything. Discover your talents and embrace them. Let yourself live based on your inborn talents, and then, things will become easier.
5. **Hito ni shinsetsu ni** - „be good for all living beings", but also work for the benefit of all living beings by embracing your talents and natural genius, gave to you by spiritual power (God, Universe, Source).

This is yet another level of deeper understanding of the Five Precepts.

***

Frans Stiene said that the most important aspect of Mikao Usui's teachings is to make our mind embrace the Five Precepts into daily life, so that each day we could live by these guidelines. In results, we will live a life without anger or worries; we will live simply and honestly, with pure compassion for all living beings. The rest of the teachings, such as meditations or symbols, are merely tools that we can use on our path towards the goal – the goal that is manifestation of the life described by the Gokai.

Gokai Practical Techniques

It's time to discuss some practical techniques for Five Precepts. On the following pages I often refer to a traditional sit of seiza, but know this: you can just as well sit down in an armchair. The rule is simple, be comfortable enough to relax, but not comfortable enough to fall asleep.

You know the basic technique already:

> Each morning and each evening sit down, get comfortable, place your hands in Gassho and recite the Precepts. Do this honestly; you can whisper, and focus on each precept individually. Notice that "just for today" can be considered a Precept, as well. Usui Reiki Ryoho Gakkai practices so called Gokai Sansho. It's a practice, during which the Precepts are repeated three times in the morning and three times in the evening – but this is an optional technique. The most important thing to remember is that you should try to "feel" each of the Precepts, either spiritually or energetically, allowing the Precept to "flow" into you. You can recite the Precepts mentally or vocally.

In the morning, intend for the Precepts to manifest during the day – wish to not fall into anger, to not worry, to feel happy and grateful, to show compassion and be good for all living beings.

Then, every evening analyze your day from the perspective of the Precepts. If you got angry, contemplate upon the reasons of your anger to understand it better. If you worried about something, contemplate about the source of your worries. It is said that when unconscious source of the problems become conscious, the problems are gone. If you can use the Precepts as anchors to contemplate upon your problems, this will offer you deeper understanding of yourself and it will allow you to free yourself from the unconscious sources of your daily problems.

> In the old days, the students of Buddhism used to write down the teachings passed on to them by the teacher. The

process of writing is one of the techniques helping to understand the teachings. Thus, you may wish to write down your own copy of the Precepts. Don't print it, but write it down with your own hand and a pen, and place this copy somewhere accessible, like in your bedside table. You can write the Precepts in English, or traditionally with Japanese and Chinese symbols.

The Usui Reiki Ryoho Gakkai practices the following meditation, too. It is called Nantatsu Ho.

Sit in seiza and focus your sight on the floor in front of you. Relax your body and mind, and then place your hands in Gassho. Now, place one of your hands on your forehead, and second hand on the back of your head. While keeping your hands there, keep reciting the Precepts for five minutes. Do this honestly. When you're done, take one hand from your forehead and place it on your Hara (abdomen), while keeping the second hand still on the back of your head. Sit like this for a while and relax. When you're done, place your hands in Gassho again for a minute or two.

You can meditate with each of the Precepts. To do so, first choose the Precept that you wish to meditate with.

Sit in seiza and focus your sight on the floor in front of you. Place your hands in Gassho and relax. Breath normally. After a while, place your hands on your knees. Continue to breath normally and focus your mind on your inner self, freeing yourself from thoughts and daily issues.

Next, think about the chosen Precept. Keep thinking about it for a while, and then, allow thoughts, emotions, feelings and memories to show themselves in your mind, as related to the chosen precept. Observe these thoughts, emotions etc, for a while. Then, use visualization to relate all these thoughts to the Precept itself in positive manner. For example, if you meditate with the second Precept, and you recalled some worries, try to contemplate upon these worries to see the positive side of them.

When you feel you're done, and you wish to end the meditation, place your hands in Gassho again.

Another technique is a simple practice of contemplation. You can contemplate all the Precepts, or you can choose a single Precept to work with. Contemplation is something between meditation and daily life. For a Western person, I often recommend contemplation mixed with relaxation.

Prepare the environment. Play some relaxing music in the background, light an incense or a candle, prepare yourself a cup of coffee or tea. Generally, do anything that will help you relax for half an hour. Make sure no one will disturb you. Then choose the Precept to work with and begin to contemplate it. Soon, in response to the Precept, you will recall thoughts, memories or experiences that you can contemplate upon, as well.

Such contemplation, thinking about your own life, allows you to understand yourself better, discover your intentions and motivations, or even sources of your behavior. The relaxing and safe environment, on the other hand, allows you to heal and release the unpleasant emotions or thoughts.

Let this practice of spiritual healing be a part of your daily, real life. Because working with the Precepts is meant to give results in your daily, real life. The Reiki Precepts are an integral part of the Reiki practice. At least some of the techniques explained above should be practiced as part of your regular Reiki practice.

Four Symbols and Jumons

Another important Element of Reiki is a set of four symbols and their names – jumons. The symbols are another example of integral part of Reiki system, often neglected by the practitioners. Sometimes symbols are considered to be unimportant, weak add-ons, that should be rejected at some point of practice. Unfortunately, some practitioners reject the symbols before they can actually learn the power of these symbols. And the symbols are very powerful tools that are an important part of the second and third degree of Reiki, respectively Okuden and Shinpiden. In this chapter I will discuss the essence of working with the symbols. Deeper understanding of the symbols will be described in the final chapter of this book.

I should already mention that in accordance to Carl Jung, one of the reason why people use symbols in general is the capability to enclose complex concepts within the symbols, concepts that are sometimes too complex or too difficult to describe them with words. On some level, Reiki symbols are in agreement with this statement. Reiki symbols represent spiritual ideas and concepts that are too large and too complex to be enclosed with single phrase. As such, symbols allow the practitioner to connect with spiritual forces and concepts, and with the practitioner's inner self as well – and with Buddha's nature, in the end. By working with the symbols we can feel their strength, their „energies", colors and feelings that are associated with these symbols. By doing so, we make steps towards rediscovering our true nature.[80] Finally, as Frans Stiene put it, Reiki practitioner do not use the symbol – the practitioner becomes that which the symbol represents.

Symbols in Far East Tradition

Reiki Symbols (Reiki Shirushi) are a form of Shuji (a „seed") - in the tradition of esoteric Buddhism in Japan (Tendai and Shingon) the Shuji, originating from Siddham[81], are associated with deities and spiritual beings. The Shuji are meant to carry the spiritual power of the particular spiritual being. The Shuji are sacred symbols, often called an „alphabet of Buddhas". Directly, only the SHK symbol is truly a Siddham symbol, originating from the Hrih symbol, associated with Buddha Amida. All the other three symbols are only theoretically associated with Buddhist light beings. In reality, the associations do not exists, as we work only with Reiki energy, and not with the beings.[82]

Still, we actually work with Shuji here. Under this „seed" we won't find a spiritual being, but a set of intentions associated with the symbol. These intentions, that is the effects of the symbol, can be also described through symbolic and metaphoric relation with the spiritual beings – that is why these entities will be described in this book. In other words, the association with spiritual beings

---

80 See: http://www.ihreiki.com/blog/article/reiki_symbols

81 Siddham is a type of writing, used also as an alphabet. With it, some sutras have been written down. Some symbols are associated with spiritual powers. A popular example of Siddham character is Om. More on Siddham can be found in "The Big Book of Reiki Symbols".

82 I might be wrong, though, and the light beings may actually support Reiki practitioners :).

should be considered as symbolic explanation of intentions and effects of each Reiki symbol.

Modern „Western" schools of Reiki created a lot of modern Reiki symbols, but in the traditional practice, we work only with four symbols. They are well known in Japan – thus, the traditional symbols do not originate in Egypt, Tibet, Atlantis or any other New Age place.

Three symbols are taught on the second degree (Okuden), and the third degree (Shinpiden) teaches the final, fourth symbol. Four symbols are enough for successful and positive practice. Also, the order of learning and working with the symbols is important.

On the first degree, Shoden, the practitioner learns the absolute basics – how to work with Reiki, how to channel the energy, how to work with breathing techniques, and how to integrate the Five Precepts into daily life. When the basics have been learned, and the foundation for the future practice is built, the time for the second degree comes. Okuden introduces three symbols – they are stronger than any other previous Reiki practice, and they affect deeper levels of our being. The order of the symbols is important, too. The practice of healing must begin with working with the first symbol. This work may take from six to twelve months at least. Only then we can proceed to working with second symbol. After another six to twelve months we can face the third symbol. As you can already see, practice with the symbols may take many years.

The symbol is „made" with the actual symbol, called Shirushi, and its name, known as Jumon. Thus, we deal with the graphical aspect of the symbol and its vocal/sound aspect. Now it's a good time to define what is a mantra and how is it different from a Jumon, because mantra is not really a proper term here. Jumon is the correct term, because this word describes this particular aspect of the symbol. Jumon is a term originating from Buddhist teachings: mikkyo. Jumon is a term for a phrase that has at least three syllables but it can be as long as an entire sutra. Now, mantra affects a person after a long time of practice. You need to repeat mantra multiple times to get results. On the other hand, a jumon gives results right away, you just need to repeat it three times. Jumon is a set of words or syllables that gives specific outcome and carries a spiritual power that acts here and now.

How the Symbols (Might) Work

The basic power of the symbol is enclosed within the symbol itself, as the schools of Shingon and Tendai state. But it's merely a basic power. The rest – that which can develop through working with the symbols – comes from the practitioner himself.

Japanese term „jumon" can be translated as following: *„a sound that summons particular cosmic vibration."* Sometimes jumons are called kotodama, that translates as „words carrying spirit", which is a Shinto concept. The symbol and its name, that is Shirushi and its Jumon, summons particular energies (vibrations) along with particular intentions – thus, when summoned, the symbol offers particular effects. While every jumon can be translated into a phrase that describe the meaning of the symbol, this meaning won't be complete – in reality, it will be empty. The symbol and the jumon must summon particular cosmic energetic vibration – translating the name of the symbol should be considered mainly a trivia.

Because every symbol carries a particular vibration, first two symbols summon particular energies (Earth Ki and Heaven Ki), and second two symbols shape a particular state of mind. Reiki symbols reach the depths of human being, the heart and the soul and the mind, allowing the practitioner to explore his inner self and rediscover Buddha's nature. Working with the symbols develops our grounding and intuition, and by doing so, beings to shape the state of balance. While Shoden degree is mainly about building a foundation for spiritual growth, the Okuden is an actual first step on the spiritual path.

It must be stated that the symbols do not „do" many things popularized by books on Reiki. For example, the first symbol do not give spiritual protection, and the second symbol do not heals karma. Such effects – additional uses for symbols – are a side effects of working with the symbols. The protection happens because we develop our grounding. The healing of karma happens because we rediscover our Buddha's nature. And so on, so on.

Stienes point out to the words of Liu I Ming. In XIX century, Ming said that as time passed, people became too focused on the symbols themselves. Confucians neglected them as pointless; Taoists focused too much on mystical and complex meanings.[83] Back to Reiki, as we look at all these modern uses for Reiki, effects and keywords associated with Reiki symbols, we may get lost in all of this. Thus, if we wish to truly experience a real effect of working with the symbols, we need to focus on actual work with the symbols, and not on the multiple uses of these symbols as described in popular Wester literature.

Hiroshi Doi, a well-known Reiki scholar, said that Reiki symbols are like additional wheels by child's bike, and that at some point, these additional wheels are no longer necessary. But Hiroshi Doi stated, just as many other Reiki masters did, that we should not get rid of the symbols too soon. We should give them up when the time is right – when we understand what these symbols stand for, and when we finally develop Reiki to a specific point – and we can develop Reiki to that point only through working with the symbols. Then, the symbols will „walk away" on their own, when

---

83 Stiene, B., Stiene F., *Japanese Art of Reiki*, p. 127.

their job will be finished. But this practice can take many years –
10, 15, 20, perhaps even 40 perhaps.

Reiki Symbols – a Metaphor of the Evolution of Human Soul

One of my teachers, Arkadiusz Lisiecki, told me that the symbols
can be seen as a map for human enlightenment and the evolution
of a human soul. The journey with the symbols begins with CKR,
that summons Reiki energy, allowing it to become a part of our life
again, and become a part of our body, mind and heart. Reiki energy
manifests itself and begins the process of healing. After some time,
we move to working with the second symbol, the SHK, and we
plant a seed of enlightenment, a seed of harmony, and a seed of
highest consciousness. It's like planting a small tree that, if we
attend it well, will grow big, into an enlightened nature of Buddha.
Working with the second symbol strengthens the seed.

As we move to working with the third symbol, we begin to feel
connection with the higher consciousness, with the Great White
Light, and we begin to slowly reach our Buddha's nature. The third
symbol itself can be pictured as the tree that grows slowly but
steadily. Arkadiusz Lisiecki relates this to a Bodhi tree, under
which the historical Buddha achieved enlightenment. Finally, when
we begin our work with the fourth symbol, strong energy flows
onto us, and it lights the fire of enlightenment on the top of our
spiritual tree. This fire radiates with harmony and Unity.

In the four symbols we perceive a closed cycle. We first allow
the spiritual energy to establish itself within us, and we progress
with the practice until the light of enlightenment is lighted. In
Japan, in traditional Reiki practice, the fourth symbol – DKM – is
considered not just a tool for practice, but also a symbol of the
final goal: achieving the state of Buddha, becoming one with the
Great White Light.

The path to enlightenment and healing is an integral element of Reiki essence.

***

On the next pages I will describe the symbols, exploring their traditional, symbolic and spiritual meaning.

Choku Rei

Choku Rei is the first Reiki symbol. These days, this symbol is often associated with power or strength. Many of the modern sources limits the use of CKR to strengthening other symbols or „channeling" huge amounts of Reiki energy to a specific place and time. Such modern uses are actually working and they are useful – they work for both CKR and for other Reiki symbols, too. But the point of this book is to present a more traditional and deeper spiritual understanding of the symbols, so that's what we're going to do.

Choku Rei is the symbol that opens and begins the practice with the symbols. As such, it build a strong foundation for the future spiritual practice.

Spiritual Meaning of Choku Rei Practice

Traditionally, this symbol is related to focus and concentration. Working with this symbol builds foundation for future growth and healing. It's the symbol that we start with when working with Okuden. This work should take at least six months. In a way, this practice continues what Shoden started. The symbol develops our grounding and foundation, upon which healthy and safe spiritual practice can be built.

First two symbols – *Choku Rei* and *Sei Heki* – shape the Ki energy within us, both the Earth Ki and Heaven Ki. Two other symbols – *Hon Sha Ze Sho Nen* and *Dai Ko Myo* – will later on shape spiritual states of mind. While it's an over simplification, it should be encoded in your memory that first two symbols work with energies, second two symbols work with state of mind. It will help you with understanding the symbols later.

First symbol and its jumon „summons" and affect earth energy, that is Earth Ki. It's the first of Three Diamonds. This energy is „heavy", which should be understood as grounding energy that is strong.

Terms such as „summoning" or affecting are not really about actual attraction of some energies from unknown place, but about developing these energies that are already within us. By working with the Choku Rei, we strengthen the Hara (in abdomen). This results in strengthening our connection with our primal energy, passed on to us by our parents (it's a Taoist concept), and strengthening the connection with everything that is of earth. We also heal everything that is related either to down-to-earth stuff, or to the idea of In (Yin).

This symbol also grounds and embraces beliefs, truths and opinions that are good for us, that helps us remain steady in our life. This can be related to strength that helps us deal with life problems, or to strengthening our point of view and opinions that help us remain free of other people's manipulations.

The Source of the Symbol

Choku Rei is associated with the cosmology of the Tendai school,[84] and it's related to old Buddhist texts of this school. This symbol can be found, either as a whole or in parts, on the walls of temples in Japan. In Tendai tradition, we encounter similar symbols that represent the element of Earth (as an elemental force of nature). A Spiral itself – a part of CKR – used to symbolize unity and harmony between forces of earth and heaven.

This symbol can be described with the words like „Focus" and „Concentration" in Japanese schools of Reiki.

We can find sources of this symbol in the tradition of Shinto, as well. A Kanji for the word „Choku" is used in a Shinto ritual of cleansing (misogi) – in the concept of spiritual healing, this word suggests honesty.[85] Thus, working with this symbol may also affect our honesty in life, or in work, or in relations with other people, but mainly honesty with ourselves.

Choku Rei and Hara

The first symbol of Reiki is associated with the abdomen

---

84 Ibidem, p. 124.

85 Ibidem, p. 93.

dantien, that is Hara. This symbol develops our connection with the first Diamond, the Ki energy of Heaven.

Daiseishi Bosatsu and Choku Rei

A spiritual being associated with this symbol is Daiseishi Bosatsu. The name of this entity is translated as „One who walks forward with great strength." Generally, this Bodhisattva will help every person to awake Buddha's nature that allows the person to walk towards enlightenment. He will do so through wisdom.

Daiseishi Bosatsu is one of the Bodhisattvas. He is shown on paintings carrying a blossoming lotus flower in his left hand, while his right hand represents vital forces that allow the flower to grow. In total, this represents a power that leads to enlightenment and awakening of higher intentions.

In Buddhist traditions it is said that he is one of the Bodhisattvas that accompany the great Buddha Amida, along with Bodhisattva Avalokiteśvara. While Avalokiteśvara carries an infinite compassion, Daiseishi Bosatsu carries the infinite wisdom.

He uses his strength to awake wisdom in people, thus allowing them to enter the path leading towards enlightenment. At the same time, he protects people from leaving this path for mere hate, fears or lower emotions. The strength of this Bodhisattva allows the person to see through illusions and suffering, to defeat these low emotions through wisdom, that helps the person to distinguish good from evil, and walk the path of Buddha.

This is reflected in the symbol of Choku Rei. Daiseishi Bosatsu is a symbol here – his characteristic and strength is seen in the first symbol. By working with the CKR, the practitioner begins to awake inner wisdom and ability to distinguish between the real world and the world of illusion. Thus, the practitioner enters the path of Buddha. At the same time, the practitioner develops the ability to protect himself against „bad" path, that is: negative emotions, fears, evil intentions, and falling into a trap of aggression, hate and negative stress.

Sei Heki

The second symbol of Reiki is Sei Heki. These days, the symbol is often associated with the concept of bringing harmony back and healing energetic blockages that allow us to achieve balance in our life. This symbol is often associated with the mental healing or healing of bad habits. But this is just a small piece of the entire puzzle.

The second symbol can be described with a word „harmony". It develops our connection with the second Diamond, that is the Ki energy of Heaven, and by doing so, it brings inner harmony back. A spiritual being associated with this symbol is Amida Nyorai, a Buddha of Infinite Light. He transforms desire and lust into wisdom and higher feelings.

Let's return for a moment to the matter of mental healing. In order to understand how this symbol is related to the process of mental healing, once again we have to see the sources and Buddhist affiliation of this symbol. Mikao Usui, when talking about Reiki, said:

> (…) First we have to heal our spirit. Secondly we have to keep our body healthy. If our spirit is healthy and conformed to the truth, body will get healthy naturally.[86]

What he says is that mind is the source of every illness. Healing the mind leads to healing the body. These teachings were passed from Usui to Chujiro Hayashi to Chiyoko Yamaguchi.

Sei Heki Chiryo, known in the West as the mental healing, is in reality, as translation states, „a healing method to heal bad habits". Bad habits in this context are fears, lust, desires, false beliefs, traumas but also, as some may say, bad karma. All of this is affected through the second symbol.

Spiritual Meaning for Sei Heki Practice

While the first symbol summoned and developed our connection with the Earth Ki, the second symbol develops our Heaven Ki. Earth Ki is heavy, grounding and protective. Opposite to this, Heaven Ki is light, and it embraces our spirituality. Sei Heki symbolizes return to harmony and rediscovering of the true nature of things. By working with the second symbol, we develop our intuition and the connection with our own spirit (soul), the source of spiritual power.

When we return to the state of harmony, for example by working

---

86 http://www.reiki.nu/reiki/interview/interview.html

with this symbol, we release all unwanted Shadows that hide within our body and mind. But traditionally, this symbol is not related to bad addictions, but to false perception of the world and beliefs and behaviors, that are not in harmony with the state of Buddha's nature.

By working with this symbol, we get closer to achieving the state of the mind that allows us to work with the next symbol – HS.

The Source of the Symbol

This symbol originates from the Siddham script. In Sanskrit, this symbol is called Hrih, and in Japan it is called Kiriku. Hrih/kiriku is a seed syllable, a term you should already be familiar with – Shuji, a seed of growth. Symbols like this are often used in esoteric Buddhism of China and Japan for the purpose of meditation. Traditionally, such symbol is painted and hanged on a wall in the meditation chamber, so that a person can focus on the symbol and "meditate on the symbol".

At first, seed symbols represented no idea or concept, but a sound that carried a particular value or virtue. After some time, symbols were associated with the sounds to create the seeds.[87]

Traditionally in Japan, the Hrih symbol was carved in a stone or wood and it was placed in the northern part of the land or city, directing the symbol towards South. This way, the symbol was meant to provide spiritual protection of the land it was facing.

Sei Heki and the Head

The second symbol is associated with the second Diamond and the head dantien. Working with this symbol develops our connection with the Heaven energies.

---

87 Stiene, B., Stiene F., *Japanese Art of Reiki*, p. 97.

Amida Nyorai and Sei Heki

Spiritual being associated with this symbol is Amida Nyorai. He is a main deity of the Pure Land Buddhism. As you may know, Mikao Usui was a practitioner of the Pure Land school. Some practices of this school are in use by the Tendai, with which Usui was familiar as well. Amida Nyorai is a Buddha of Infinite Compassion that offers spiritual peace of mind and body.

Amida Buddha is often presented as sitting in lotus position, on a lotus flower, keeping his hands in a mudra of meditation.

He is a Buddha directly associated with Pure Land school. He is also known as a Buddha of Infinite Light. His light of wisdom and enlightenment radiates the entire Universe. Also, his compassion for all living beings is infinite.

This Buddha never turns his back on bad or evil people. No matter what „sins" a person committed, this Buddha offers a chance for enlightenment. It is a legend that ninja warriors and unpleasant people worshiped this Buddha in hope or being reborn in his „paradise", where they could experience spiritual cleansing, and in return, be reborn in a better human body that would allow them to achieve enlightenment.

In a symbolic meaning, all of this means that working with the second symbol is meant and is available to every living begin. No matter what bad things you may have done in the past, you can enter the path that leads to enlightenment.

***

First two symbols represent Ki energies, one of earth, the other one of heaven. That is In and Yo (Yin and Yang). When these two elements merge together, they create everything that is. They create a whole that wasn't in existence before. Harmonious connection between In and Yo results in positive, happy life. Through harmony between these two elements we experience health and Unity with ourselves and the world around us.

Hon Sha Ze Sho Nen

The third symbol of Reiki is the Hon Sha Ze Sho Nen. These days, this symbol is mainly associated with being a primary tool of channeling Reiki over distance (distant healing). But this use is just a tip of an iceberg. The main role of this symbol is to prepare the mind of the practitioner and prepare the practitioner in general to walk the path leading to enlightenment. This symbol is also used to regain connection – with ourselves, the world that surrounds us, and the Buddha's nature within us.

Spiritual Meaning of Hon Sha Ze Sho Nen Practice

The third and fourth symbols of Reiki are a Kanji – Chinese

characters used in Japanese culture. Working with these two symbols leads to changing our perception of everything that is. The third symbol can be described with the word „connection". But it's not about connection during distant healing. It's more about becoming aware of our connection to everything that is – realizing that we are part of the Universe, and the Universe is a part of us. When we finally experience this fact, then we can learn how to live in harmony with the cycles of the Universe. We become one with the Universe. The symbol itself can be read as **"Right consciousness is the source of everything"**. Spiritual being associated with this symbol is Bodhisattva Avalokiteśvara, also known as Kannon. This being hears the problems of the world and helps solving them.

Working with this symbol shapes a particular state of mind. A State of connection and unity with everything that is.

Many authors, scholars and speakers these days talk about the feeling of separation – most people these days feel separated from the reality that surrounds them. Working with the HS helps us regain this feeling of connection; connection we never actually lost. In result, we improve our sense of self-worth, and the awareness of worth of other things and people, as well as we develop compassion for all living beings. We never lost the connection with the world, we just forgot that we were connected. Working with this symbol helps us remember this connection. The sense of connection is an important concept associated with Buddhism, Shinto and Shugendo.

But before we begin to remember this connection, we need to reach the state of harmony between Earth and Heaven energies by working with the first two symbols.

Additional knowledge can be gained by looking at the many translations of the symbol: „my primal nature is a right thought",

„I am the right awareness","The right awareness is the source of everything", „Through right thought and right meditation, a man discovers the real Self" - these are some of the translations, of which meaning is very similar to each other. By studying this symbol, we begin to discover that the practice with HS leads us to discovering our true nature – the nature of Buddha, the real „Self", the primal nature filled with goodness, love and wisdom. It's an important state on the path to achieving the state of Unity.

By working with the third symbol, we develop our intuition, and we open the gates to inspiration and signs from the Universe, or Spirits, or God. These signs lead us on our individual path of spiritual growth. They lead us to developing our talents and reaching the state of Unity.

This symbol opens the gates to achieving the Buddha's nature.

The Source of the Symbol

HS is the only Reiki symbol that does not have real sources, and, most probably, was created entirely by Mikao Usui for the purpose of Reiki. HS is made of five classic Kanji, that were put together by Usui in order to create a new symbol, that can be read as a normal sentence. Usui used spiritual practices of esoteric Buddhism and Shinto to create this symbol and give it its spiritual meaning for Reiki practice.

Hon Sha Ze Sho Nen and the Heart

HS is associated with the second dantien, the one in the Heart. Here, energies of Heaven and Earth come together, this is where we achieve the state of harmony between ourselves and the world around us.

The Heart is a metaphor here, a symbolic key to the doors of happiness and harmony. This happiness and harmony can be experienced both by individual person, and by society as a whole.

When the state of Unity and connection is reached, the practitioner becomes ready to start the journey of the fourth symbol.

Kannon and Hon Sha Ze Sho Nen

Kannon, that is Bodhisattva Avalokiteśvara, is a light being associated with this symbol.

In Buddhist cosmology, Kannon is considered a spiritual son of Buddha Amida.[88] In Japan we may say that gender of this Bodhisattva has been changed, and the Goddess Kannon was born. Another name for this being is Kanzeon Bosatsu.[89] Such change of gender is nothing new nor complicated in case of Buddhist deities, because gender is considered merely a down-to-earth concept, unrelated to spiritual realms.

In Shingon tradition, Kannon hold a lotus flower in his hand, a flower being a symbol of spiritual enlightenment for all living beings. His second hand is often pictured in mudra representing lack of fears and fearless support for all living beings on their path to enlightenment.

This Bodhisattva is named to be „the one who hears the voice of the entire world". He made an oath to hear out all living beings and help them in freeing themselves from suffering, and helping them on the path to enlightenment, protecting all living beings from the pain of existence. To do so, Kannon can take any form – a person, an animal, or an event in life.

Through a symbolic meaning, the work with the third symbol suggests that it's a symbol helping us walk the path towards enlightenment. It helps us develop our true nature (Buddha's nature), recognize evil and suffering around us, and within us as

---

88 Tubielewicz, J., *Mitologia Japonii*, p. 174.

89 Williams, P., *Buddyzm Mahajana*, . 284.

well, and defeat that which is evil. To do so, the HS place multiple people and events on our life path so that with their help, we can discover ourselves and our true nature.

Dai Ko Myo

The final symbol of Reiki is the Dai Ko Myo. The practitioner learns this symbol once on the third degree, Shinpiden. These days, we consider this symbol to be a „master symbol", which role is to attune other people to Reiki, but just like in case of previous symbols, DKM has a lot deeper spiritual meaning.

DKM is a powerful meditation symbol, a crown jewel on the path of working with the symbols. But at the same time, it's merely the first step on another stage of spiritual journey towards harmony and enlightenment.

Spiritual Meaning of Dai Ko Mo Practice

It's another symbol that develops a specific state of mind – one related to enlightenment, helping us manifest our true nature.

To fully experience the beauty of Reiki, we need to walk through all three stages and work hard with all Five Elements. Only then we're capable of reaching deeply into the nature of Reiki. Devotion, time, patience, work, effort and discipline – all of this is required to experience Reiki fully.

DKM is made of three separate Kanji that translate as „Great White Light".

The practice with this symbol leads to achieving the state of Unity. But don't be mislead, it's a symbol that finalize the practice, but in order for it to work effectively, we must work with it for many years. And that must be preceded by long years of work with previous symbols and meditation techniques.

Working with this symbol also „lights up the heart", meaning that DKM makes our inner spiritual strength greater over time. This spiritual power then radiates onto all living beings. But don't be mislead, again. Mikao Usui achieved Satori first, only then Reiki flew into him – this is how the Reiki method has been created. Before a Reiki practitioner reaches the final stage of Reiki path and understands this power, he must first achieve the state of harmony, then the state of Satori, and only then, the state of enlightenment and finally, Unity.

DKM does not have a specific area of the body associated with it. Just like the CKR is associated with Hara, SHK with the head and HS with the heart, DKM have no such reference area. DKM leads to integrating together the elements of body and spirit, enlightening the entire human being.

The Source of the Symbol

The symbol itself is very popular in many parts of Japan. It's a symbol of enlightenment and is well known in Buddhism of Japan. Even on the Mount Kurama itself we can find this character.

DKM can be discovered in Mikkyo teachings of the Tendai school, too. According to which, in one of the practices, the symbol is used to integrate the practitioner with the Great White Light, represented by Dainichi Nyorai, Buddha of the Great Light. Integration with this Light that begins to manifest through the practitioner, opens the path towards enlightenment.

Also, another Japanese traditions use this symbol to represent the final concept of Unity, enlightenment and Great White Light; including martial arts, Shugendo and other Buddhist schools.

Dainichi Nyorai and Dai Ko Myo

Dainichi Nyorai is a light being associated with this symbol. He is the Buddha of the Great Light. His spiritual power light everything that is. It disperses darkness, gives life and spiritual nourishment to all living beings.

He is the main Buddha in Shingon tradition.

Dainichi Nyorai is known as the great Cosmic Buddha, Buddha Vairocana. It is said that Dainichi Nyorai disperse darkness and enlightens all things; allows things to happen; is a light that cannot be unmade.[90]

According to Shingon school, this Buddha is a manifestation of Compassion and Wisdom. He's also a symbol of self-knowledge and self-awareness of the Universe. In a way, it's related to the „intelligence" and „awareness" given to Reiki energy, too.

Dainichi Nyorai is considered to be a manifestation of the Great White Light, and in result, with Reiki energy. Still we must

---

90 M. Kiyota, Shingon Buddhism..., p. 61, [IN:] Kosior, K., *Budda*, p. 132.

remember that we're talking about symbolic meaning here.

If you remember the history of Mikao Usui (not mentioned in this book, though), you may recall that it was the vision of Buddha Vairocana, that made Usui begin his spiritual search.

Dainichi Nyorai is a symbol of spiritual Unity of the Universe.[91]

This Buddha has two primary forms, represented by two different mandalas. In one of them, we find Wisdom represented by particular mudra – it's the Vajradhatu Mandala. It symbolizes the unity between all living beings and Buddhas, saying that the enlightenment and Buddha's nature is available to everyone of us. Another form of this Buddha represents Great Light, which is the source of everything that is. It's a metaphor of saying that we are all one. It's the Garbhakosa Mandala.

He is a Buddha of the Great Light. His life force lights everything that is, nourish all living beings, like a spiritual power nourishes plants, animals and people. The strength of this Buddha disperse darkness with light. It gives life and nourish all living beings. It transcend past, present and future, leading all beings to enlightenment.

Everything that is and exists, comes from this Buddha. He is the Source, the Great White Light. The source of everything that is and the place to which everything that is returns. Working with this symbol is meant to help us rediscover our connection with the Great White Light and integrate it into our daily life.

We should also mention the opposite side of Dainichi Nyorai. Many light beings in Buddhism has their opposite forms, so called wrathful deities. Their task is to destroy, burn and banish everything that is bad and evil in ourselves or in our life. While these deities may look scary, their task is to push us forward on the path to enlightenment. In case of the fourth symbol and Dainichi

---

91 Hall, J.W., *Japonia od czasów najdawniejszych do dzisiaj*, p. 56.

Nyorai, the wrathful deity is Fudo Myoo, often pictured as surrounded by flames. He deals with lust, bad desires, ignorance, greed, anger and injustice. He fights fears. All of this so that we can walk forward on the path to enlightenment.

Fudo Myoo supports the practitioner on the path of discipline and self-control, using his sword of wisdom. Any wrathful deities forms of previous light beings are not that present in the practice of Reiki – of course, in symbolic meaning. But the truth is that working with the fourth symbol may result in experiences similar to Fudo Myoo shaking his sword, fighting through your ignorance, fears and hate.

The fourth symbol can be described with a word of „becoming". With practice, we become one, and the line between „Self" and „Reiki" disappears. Like in the teachings of Usui, practitioner and Reiki becomes one.

Integration of the Three Diamonds and the Reiki Symbols

I mentioned already that first two symbols points out to energy, two later symbols points out to a state of mind. Working with these symbols in correct order offers us a steady spiritual growth and self-healing. We begin our practice with working out the first symbol, CKR, that develops our inner Chi, our grounding and builds up the foundation for future grow. Then, we work with the second symbol, the SHK, that starts the process of healing of our emotions and mind, clearing both from things that stop us from achieving the state of harmony.

Next, we work with the third symbol, the HS, that begins to shape a proper state of mind for spiritual practice, thanks to first two symbols clearing the path. Then, the room for true spiritual growth is prepared, so that we can begin our work with the fourth symbol, the DKM, that integrates the previous symbols and their effects together.

All of this is clearly visible in the symbolics of the final symbol. The top Kanji represents a man. The middle Kanji is fire, and bottom Kanji represents moon and the sun – a universal symbol for In and Yo (Yin and Yang). The entire symbol shows the process of integration of these elements. Just like these elements pursuit harmony, so is the Reiki practitioner working to achieving inner and outer harmony.

Working with the symbols should take at least two years. It doesn't mean that we will heal everything that must be healed during these two years. Your work with the symbols can be repeated and continued. This will be discussed soon.

Treatments and Self-Treatments

Another Element of Reiki is the practice of treatments and self-treatments. These are the practices that are most popular these days and are associated with Reiki in the Western world. A keyword here is a Japanese term „*Tenohira*" - it's a term that describes healing through touch, by placing hands on specific areas of the body in a specific way (thus, for example, through hand positions, well known to Reiki practitioners). The idea behind this practice is to empower and support the the flow of Ki energy by „radiating" Reiki from our hands into the particular part of the body.

The goal of this practice is to increase the amount of Ki that flows within the body. That means we replenish the shortages of energy, and we clean the energy, increasing the quality of this life force within us. The Reiki energy enters the body and is distributed to areas of the body that really need this energy. Placing the hands in particular part of the body also helps us deal with energy blockages in the body, like a needle deals with them in case of acupuncture. Also, we can improve our ability to deal with energetic blockages by learning and developing the technique of Byosen Reikan Ho, a technique of sensing the energetic blockages within the body. That said, before you proceed to Byosen Reikan Ho, you should still learn the guidelines regarding hand positions, because they often come in handy when you're still a beginner.

Spiritual Aspects of Working with Tenohira

I find it interesting when teachings Reiki to use particular terms to describe the entire practice of treatments. Reiki practitioner is not a healer – he's a **practitioner**. He does not heal – it's the Reiki energy that **supports the body** of the receiver, and it's the body that heals itself. Furthermore, Reiki practitioner do not send energy. He merely **opens** himself for the flow of Reiki and **allows** the energy to flow through him. It's the body of the receiver that actually **draws** the energy and directs it wherever it needs and in such amounts it needs.

That is why the practitioner of Reiki do not have any control over the results of Reiki treatment. When you approach the treatment, you just open for the flow of Reiki. The „size of opening" and the quality of the energy depends on how much time you spent on your personal spiritual practice, and to what degree you healed your mind and heart. The person receiving Reiki also opens for the flow of this energy, allowing himself or herself to receive this energy, and receiver's body (as well as mind and soul) decides, where the energy is needed. This is how a channel is opened from both ends – the receiver is open and draws the energy, and the practitioner of Reiki is open, and channels the energy. But neither the receiver nor the practitioner decides what will get healed and in what way. Reiki brings harmony back and creates the entire process of healing.

Placing our hands on the body has a symbolic meaning, as well.

By touching the person, we connect with this person. The touch is like a symbol of connection, and a symbol of acquiescence for the treatment. It's also a symbolic spiritual agreement for contact with another spiritual being and the goodness flowing from this person. When the touch deals with physical barriers, the mind barrier is the last to fall. The receiver deals with this final blockage by opening for the flow of Reiki. And the practitioner deals with those mind barrier by giving up his own goals and intentions, and by just allowing the Reiki to flow without control over the flow.

You may notice yet another spiritual aspects of doing Reiki to other people. When we give up the need to do Reiki just for money (yes, it happens – it's a thing to heal), and we give up the idea of considering Reiki a form of business career, we begin to offer Reiki out of pure good will – then, in result, we begin to discover the beauty of Reiki practice. We may learn to connect with the other person – not necessary someone we know – and offer spiritual love and compassion to this person. This way, we support the healing of both this person and us. Understanding this, and then experiencing this, is a great spiritual gift, another proof that we are all one and connected.

Then, we also discover the strength and power of pure and honest intentions. Of course, in order to reach this state, we must spend a couple of years on our own spiritual practice.

In addition, Tenohira is a way to develop our ability to let go and give up things that are no longer needed in our life. We may, for example, wish to heal our social life. But for the purpose of healing, we need to let go of this intention, so that Reiki can deal with more urgent things to heal. It doesn't mean that this intention we let go won't be healed. It just means that this aspect of our life will have to wait in a „queue”.

Of course, working with treatments and self-treatments leads to healing our heart and mind, because we still work with Ki energy, and this energy, as it flows through our body, may heal our wounds, fears or bad memories, as it was described in this book already.

Another thing for self-Tenohira is the fact that we spend 15 to 60 minutes with ourselves – it's our personal time for intimacy with ourselves. It's not ego – it's self-love. Because we need to learn how to take care of ourselves and we need to learn how to love our own body and life, if we ever wish to learn how to love and care for other people.

And then, when we offer treatment for another person, in addition a small healing happens on a subconscious level for this person, because the receiver experiences love and care coming from you. This is very important as well.

While we deal with these spiritual aspects of the practice, it doesn't change the fact that we can give ourselves (or someone else) a very quick Reiki treatment while sitting in front of a TV, or traveling in bus. You don't have to give this up just to be a more traditional Reiki practitioner. That said, the most effective treatment is the one that is approached in the right way. Obviously, the environment must be prepared. It's more about making it safe and peaceful than mystical. You don't have to light candles or incenses if you don't feel the need to do so. These are optional things. But you need to make sure you feel safe in your environment and you're comfortable, and that you have enough peaceful time just for yourself.

Performing the Treatment

A Reiki treatment can be performed while sitting or lying down. And when you sit, you can either sit in an armchair, or in lotus or seiza sit, whichever works better for you. You may wish to set a daily schedule of treatments, that should be performed each day. Make it your daily routine to do self-Reiki. You should be familiar with a concept of 21 days of cleansing after attunements – it's quite possible that it is a modern addition, even if it relates to Tendai and Shugendo practices. While 21 days are not truly traditional, in the modern Western world, they do the trick: they teach the practitioner discipline and routine when it comes to performing Reiki daily.

The amount of time you spend on each hand position should be based on your own intuition, just like the area of the body, where you put your hands. When you're a beginner, you should stick to the hand positions described in guidebooks or practice manuals, and devote 3 to 5 minutes for each individual hand position. But then, as you progress with your inner growth, you automatically develop your intuition. Intuition, the inner voice, will later on direct our hands and intentions towards particular and right area of the body. When deep inside we feel that we should change the hand position, time of position or intention, we should follow this feeling. This is when Reiki flows at its best.

The hands themselves can take any forms. In most cases, we hold our fingers together, creating a flat surface with our palms. When we place our hands on the body, we may put one of our hands on another, and channel Reiki this way. Or, we may place both our hands side by side. We may bend our little and ring fingers, as well as our thumb, keeping our index and middle fingers straight, creating an „arrow" directing the flow of Reiki to pointed part of the body. You can „hug" the part of the body you wish to send Reiki into. Finally, we may place our hands in two different parts of the body at the same time. Of course, in all these situations, your hands may actually touch the body, or just „hover" an inch or two about the body.

When you channel Reiki, whether it's treatment or self-treatment, breathe to your Hara. Gassho meditation and Joshin Kokyu Ho may come in handy here. Hara breathing heals the physical body and the mind; it improves the flow of energy, providing an additional meditation aspect to the entire practice of Tenohira. The mind focused on the breath slows down, lets go of unnecessary thoughts, and increases the amount of Reiki flowing.

Physical feelings – things you feel physically during the treatment – are not important. Actually, not every practitioner is able to sense anything physically. We recognize whether Reiki flows and works by noticing long-term effects, and not by observing short-term physical reactions. Kathleen Prasad said once we may be able to recognize the flow of Reiki by noticing a deeper state of relaxation and focus, a meditative-like state. And we recognize the end of the flow by slowly returning to „normal", leaving the calm, relaxed state of mind. Still, it's just one of many concepts.

If it happens that you actually feel something physically, never associate it with health issues. Sometimes you may experience a pain in some area of the body; or something will sting you etc, and we may, in result, jump to wrong conclusions and panic. But don't worry about it – it's one of the many situations when we need to learn to let go – especially let go of our own fears and worries.

A problematic issue is the belief that Reiki treatment should give no negative results. A thing or two must be said here. It's true that Reiki treatment should not „suck" you out of energy. But Reiki treatment may – during the treatment itself, or some hours/days after – result in bad mood or feeling of poisoning. This suggests that Reiki works and the body initiated his self-healing mechanisms.

Head Treatment

If you wish, you may perform a treatment focused on the head of the person, the head being a center for thoughts and mind, affecting the body. The length of such treatment may vary from a few minutes to a couple dozen of minutes. But the best thing to do is to follow our own intuition. In this treatment, we just channel Reiki to:

1. Eyes and forehead.
2. Both temples.
3. The back of the head and forehead at the same time.
4. Both sides of the neck.
5. The tip of the head.

After the treatment, we may finish the practice, or direct our hands down the body, and perform an intuition-based treatment.

The above technique can be performed both on the self, or on another person. In that second case, it's recommended for that person to sit on a chair. According to Usui's teachings, the mind is the source of all illness. When we heal the mind, we heal the rest of the body, as well.

Gedoku Ho Technique

It's a detoxification technique that supports removal of toxins from the body, whether their physical or emotional. It's a simple technique, in which we channel Reiki both to Hara and to the head. To perform this technique, sit down, relax and open yourself for the flow of Reiki.

1. Place one of your hands on the Hara and focus your mind on the abdomen. This way, you connect yourself with your

primal nature.

2. Place your other hand on the forehead, connecting with your mind. Remain in this position for five minutes, channeling Reiki at the same time.

3. Now move your hand from the forehead to the Hara. Both hands are now placed on your abdomen. Focus your mind in this region, and remain relaxed for 10 to 20 minutes, channeling Reiki no more.

Byosen Reikan Ho

Byosen Reikan Ho, a traditional Reiki practice, is a technique of sensing areas of the body that suffer from energetic imbalance. These are the places where Reiki energy should be channeled. Byosen Reikan Ho is based on your own intuition and feelings that you experience when moving your hands over the body. Byosen Reikan Ho is the full name of the technique, but the word „Byosen" itself is an important thing to discuss – generally, Byosen is the actual physical feeling that you experience in your hands.

Byosen is what we feel at particular area of the body. It can be both a feeling of energy that is blocking the part of the body; and a feeling that is the body's response to the energy being sent into the body.

For example, a strong Byosen feeling can be a signal of strong energetic blockage, but also a strong reaction of the body to healing this blockages through Reiki.

To simplify things, I usually say that Byosen is the feeling that is different from how you feel the rest of the body. Into this „different" region of the body, we send Reiki – simple. But in Japan it is taught traditionally that Byosen may have five levels of intensity. These levels define the strength of the energetic blockage, from the weakest to the strongest one.

Please note: five levels of Byosen may seem like a form of diagnosis. But you cannot make a diagnosis as Reiki practitioner if you do not have proper medical training. Using the Byosen and reading the different levels of blockage's intensity is meant to help you decide how much Reiki must be sent and how many treatments must be offered before the body can return to the state of harmony. Byosen should never be used to make medical diagnosis.

Now, let's take a look at the five levels of Byosen.[92]

1. **Onnetsu – heat** – temperature or fever, or just a strong feeling of increased temperature as compared to the temperature of the rest of the body. Such feeling means that toxins were collected in small amount in this area of the body, and the energy that we're sending will allow the toxins to be healed.

2. **Atsui Onnetsu – strong heat** – it's a higher temperature than before, that may cause your hands to sweat, or you may feel like your hands are „burning". This means the amount of toxins is greater, but we can still deal with them through Reiki.

3. **Piri Piri kan** – it's a tingling sensations, like pins and needles in your hands. It may also feel like „magnetic force" either pulling your hands towards the body, or pushing them away. It may also be a feeling of your hands going numb. That last feeling of numbness should not be mistaken for lack of proper blood circulations in your hand. Piri Piri kan suggests that you're dealing not with a simple energetic blockage, but with serious lack of

---

92 Petter, *This is Reiki*, p. 192-194.

balance, that may result in later illness.

4. **Hibiki – pulsing or cold** – pulsing can be sensed as fast or slow, strong or weak, deep or shallow in terms of body's depth. But do not mistake the pulsing feeling with your own blood pulse, or another person's pulse. Cold can be also sensed that suggests even stronger imbalance of energy within the body.

5. **Itami – pain, felt in your hands** – it may be felt in your fingers, palms, wrist, or radiate further up to your elbow or even shoulder. According to Frank Petter, the pain suggests that great amount of Reiki energies flow through you in order to heal a very strong energetic blockage.

These are five main levels of Byosen sensations that you may experience while doing Reiki. You may experience them even if you're not consciously performing Byosen Reikan Ho, because they may happen to each practitioner during normal Reiki treatments.

Suggestions for Working with Byosen Reikan Ho

Now, let's share some small tips and suggestions regarding your work with Byosen – that is, sensations.

- Do not tell the person you're offering Reiki to, that his or hers energetic condition is very serious. This will cause only more troubles. If you need to say anything, just say how many treatments may be necessary to bring balance back.

- With each following treatment, Byosen sensations should be getting weaker, from level five to level one. When you can't sense anything any more, it will suggest that the blockage has been healed. But sometimes, sensations may increase due to healing crisis, but only to drop later on.

- Byosen Reikan Ho is a great tool for treatments on other people, but it can be practiced on ourselves, too.
- When your hands start to get numb, change their position a little – move your fingers, twist your wrist. If the Byosen sensation remains unchanged, it means you're sensing real Byosen; but when the sensation changes, it may mean that the way you hold your hands is blocking the blood flow.
- When you experience cold in your hands, warm them up a bit, and place them back in the place where you felt the cold. If you still feel cold, it may be Byosen – if you can't feel the cold anymore, it may suggest you just got cold.
- Sometimes, different levels of Byosen may interlace with each other, and you may sense both levels 3 and 4 at the same time, or 2 and 3 at the same time, etc. It's normal.
- If you get sensations that weren't described in the levels of Byosen, write them down in a notebook, and observe the receiver and the treatment itself. Over time, as you progress with such observation and research, you will be able to notice what these unique feelings mean to you personally.
- Remember that Byosen sensation is nothing bad, even when it's painful. Byosen is just a mean of communication between Reiki, your body and your mind.
- Sensations may come in waves. Spend at least 10 to 20 minutes for each hand position, so that you can be sure of the Byosen in that particular part of the body. At some point you may feel level 1, in a few minutes level 5, for example. Longer time for each hand position allows you to heal blockages more successful. Sometimes, you may feel,

for example, level 4, then nothing for a couple of minutes, and then level 4 again. Keep doing Reiki for a few more treatments, until the sensations disappear completely.
- Byosen may not be experienced when the receiver is on medication, or is tired and his problems are hidden. In this case, just perform a few hand positions on receiver's head, and only then proceed with the Byosen Reikan Ho.
- Even when the receiver feels good on the outside, Byosen can be perceived. It's because energetic blockages manifest themselves physically only when they turn into illness. Before that happens, the blockages may be weak or hidden and they may not be perceived through physical, outside symptoms.
- In order to experience Byosen better, remember that the sensitivity of your hands increases as you practice Reiki more. Also, it's easier to sense things when your mind is calm. That's why you should practice Gassho meditation on regular basis.

This is how the practice of Byosen Reikan Ho actually looks like:

- After opening yourself to the flow of Reiki, you hover your hands an inch or two above the receiver's body, seeking the Byosen sensations – sensations that are different from the rest of the body.
- In the part of the body where you sense Byosen, you send Reiki for 15-20 minutes, or for as long as your intuition suggests to you.
- Perform the treatment on all problematic areas of the body for a couple of days, each day, until Byosen sensations

stop to appear. Only then we can be sure the blockages are gone.

After that, when Byosen can't be sensed anywhere in the body, we can tell the receiver that we can't offer him or her any more „targeted" help and all we can do is to suggest regular treatments once or twice a month, in a form of wellness practice, or we may suggest a Reiki class so that the receiver can learn to work with Reiki on his own.

Mastering the Byosen Reikan Ho may took many years, so don't give up if you're not good at this at first.

Breathing Techniques, Meditations and their Meaning

The final Element of Reiki practice is a set of breathing techniques. In Taoism it is well known that breath is directly associated with life force (*Chi, Ki*). To breathe the right way means to live the right way. Breathing results in physical, emotional and energetic reactions. When you breathe properly, your body, mind and spirit are affected. Breathing techniques in Reiki are called generally *Kokyu Ho*. Please, don't be mislead by shortness of this chapter – while there's not much to say in theory, breathing techniques are very important and offer positive results.

Breathing techniques, in the practice of Reiki, are meant to achieve a few goals. First, they teach to breathe the correct way. A correct breathing increases the amount of oxygen being supplied to the body. Second, a correct breathing helps the practitioner enter Alpha states of mind, that is meditative states of mind. Alpha state is a particular state of brainwaves, that support relaxations and self-healing. As such states progresses, releasement of unpleasant emotions and physical tensions becomes easier. Meditative states also helps to bring order to our chaotic money minds.

In Japan, there is a concept of *naga-iki*. It says that each person is born with limited number of breaths that he can make. Thus, the length of life is set in stone. Anger, fear, stress, all these things increases the number of breaths we're making, which may shorten our lifespan.[93] It's a spiritual concept, but it can be „translated" to down-to-earth terms, because indeed it is confirmed by scientific research that negative emotions affect our health and lifespan.

Breathing techniques bring relaxation and calm down the breath. When our breathing is slow, energy flows with no disruptions, nourishing the body and the mind.

In other schools of thought such as Aikido, it is said that the right, calm breathing (and breathing techniques) lead to uniting the mind with the body, and to their positive development and growth.

In great manner, breathing techniques support the flow of Ki energy in the body and strengthen the Hara region. Later on, they strengthen and cleanse the body, heart and mind, which affects the level of spiritual growth and self-healing.

Frans Stiene says that Ki breath is also a way to strengthen the ability of the body to distribute nutrients to every cell, and in releasing toxins from these cells at the same time, which results in better health.[94]

Breathing techniques as meditation techniques allow us to let go things we kept our hold to. Like traumas or bad emotions. Breathing relaxes the physical body, removes tensions, and along with that, releases emotions, worries and similar. That's why methods such as Yoga, Tai Chi Chuan, Qigong, or even long walks (and Reiki breathing techniques, too) lead to spiritual healing by

---

93   Stiene, B., Stiene F., *Japanese Art of Reiki*, p. 78.

94   Ibidem, p. 79.

releasing the negative patterns from our life.

But remember – no technique will help you if you won't approach the practice with honest intentions of self-healing.

I explained the most important aspects of the breathing techniques. The techniques themselves will be described in the next chapter.

The Practice of Three Degrees

After discussing the theory, in this chapter we will bring everything together, so that the actual practice of Reiki can be understood well, thus prove to be effective.

The goal of this book is to help the practitioners of Reiki understand the deeper aspects of this method of self-healing. Mikao Usui created a universal technique, that can be learned by anyone. Everyone can practice Reiki. In addition, everyone can learn the deeper understanding of this method. Yet of course, most people will prefer the basic aspects of this practice. That's why Reiki **is** universal, because it allows people to get positive results with the basic and simplest techniques.

Many people just practice self-treatment and think about Five Precepts and their role in their life. This is what I teach to most of my own students as a basic package. The results of this basic approach are wonderful!

But, this book has a simple goal: to understand Reiki more than it is necessary for successful practice.

A question appears: what if you're already an Okuden or even Shinpiden practitioner, and yet you never practiced any of the advanced Reiki techniques? Well – the best thing to do is to imagine you're a Shoden practitioner again, and start from the beginning. It won't hurt. And it's actually very important, because if you're already a Shinpiden person, and yet you never tried any traditional technique of Shoden or Okuden, then you cannot just jump into advanced Shinpiden practice without working out the basics of the first and second degree. The order of the degrees is very important. The practice of Shoden prepares us for Okuden, and the practice of Okuden prepares us for Shinpiden. You cannot jump to Shinpiden stuff without dealing with Shoden and Okuden first, because without this, some very important foundation won't be created in your life. Such rush may end bad. Know this:

> One who walks slowly can clearly see the path that lies ahead.

First Degree: Shoden

The word „Shoden" means „first teachings". It's a good term to describe the practice of the first degree, which presents the basic techniques, and serves as introduction for more advanced practices. On Shoden, we deal mainly with Earth Ki and issues related to this energy. The practice of Shoden is focused on shaping and developing the following elements:

1. Growth and development the abilities of self-healing and

healing of our close friends and family through Tenohira, a formalized healing through touch and channeling healing, spiritual energy.

2. Development of the ability to sense Ki and energy – through treatment practice and Ki exercises.
3. Building the foundation for future practice by working with Hara.
4. Developing the ethics of practitioner and correct intentions for life and practice through Five Precepts.

The first point is clear. Any Reiki practice, both treatments and self-treatments, makes us better and better practitioners. At this state of practice, we should use Reiki to help ourselves, our family and our friends.

On Shoden, we're beginning the practice of self-treatments. We should spend at least 30 minutes each day doing self-treatment just like it was described in one of the previous chapters on Tenohira. But this is just the beginning.

The second point deals with techniques that develop our sensitivity for energies and spiritual matters. This sensitivity develops on its own as we progress with our daily Reiki practice. But also, we can use additional techniques and exercises to strengthen this ability, for example by learning how to sense energies of Ki. This practice will be described soon.

The third point is more complex. Just like building a house begins with building its foundation, a true spiritual growth must be started by creating a strong foundation, as well. We do this so that future, more advanced practices, won't turn out to be too difficult for us. In a way, the practice of Shoden creates a strong root system, so that we can grown a huge, strong spiritual tree.

The four point develops our perception of life and our behavior in life, by beginning the integration of the Five Precepts into our daily reality.

The practice of the first degree is focused on practicing our grounding, working with Five Precepts, and with Hara breathing techniques. As it was said earlier in this book, our work with Hara strengthens our Ki, which results in better health. Also, the Hara is associated with our subconscious, so we're beginning to heal the Heaven Diamond in a way, a Diamond related to emotions and feelings.

When we practice Shoden on regular basics, we prepare our mind and body for the future practice. We heal out negative behaviors or unhealthy diet, or even social relations etc. On Shoden, Reiki may heal also emotions, feelings and thoughts that we won't be needing in the future. All of this starts with finishing our Shoden class, and all of this creates a foundation for the future practice.

Sensing Ki – Practical Techniques

Some techniques, like Gassho Kokyu Ho meditation, can be practiced even before you begin your Shoden class. Sensing techniques can be practiced without Reiki, too. These techniques originate from Qigong practice and aren't directly associated with Reiki. They are based on working with Ki – life energy and cosmic energy. They can help the practitioner develop his sensitivity for life energies, energetic blockages and Reiki flow. You can practice these techniques for a few weeks, until you feel like they gave you positive results and actually increased your sensitivity.

It has been said already that in the practice of Reiki, we deal with three forms of Ki: Earth Ki, Heaven Ki and Heart Ki. The following are the techniques that allow us to develop our sensitivity for these forms of energy.[95]

Sensing Your Own Ki

Western Reiki manuals often recommend developing the sensitivity to energy that you can perceive through your hands. To increase this sensitivity, manuals recommend doing Reiki to your palms, and focusing on your sensations. Other teachers may suggest regular rubbing of your hands. Personally, I recommend a more Qigong-like practice, which is still quite popular in the West. This technique is not really linked to Reiki, but it can be very helpful, if you never sensed energies before, and you wish to feel them for the purpose of Reiki treatments.

Let's create a ball of Ki energy, then. Sensing this ball of energy increases the sensitivity to energies through our hands. The process of creating the ball is simple. We use visualization to visualize our Ki energy coming out from our hands, and forming a ball between our hands. So just relax, and imagine you're holding a slightly larger tennis ball between your hands. Then, visualize the Ki energy coming out from your palms, like a light, bright energy, and forming a ball of energy between your hands. Keep visualizing the ball for 5 minutes or so, and try to sense the energy between the hands. Just notice the physical and spiritual sensations between your hands, by focusing your mind on this area. When you're done, visualize as the energy of the ball loses its shape and is drawn back to your hands and into your body.

The next step is to learn simple techniques of sensing three main cosmic forces: Earth Ki, Heaven Ki and Heart Ki.

It's important to know that you should work mainly with earth and heaven energies, preferable at the same time, beginning your daily exercise with working with Earth Ki, then moving to Heaven

---

95 Stiene, *Japanese Art of Reiki*, p. 28-35.

Ki. Balance is important. Focusing only on Heaven Ki may cause emotional instability. Development of intuition and spiritual sensations may be tempting, but also dangerous for your mental health, if done the wrong way, meaning – without seeking balance between Earth and Heaven. Proper grounding is very important for the safety of spiritual growth.

Sensing Earth Ki

Earth energy is strong, powerful and very grounded. The technique that allows us to sense Earth Ki is, at the same time, a grounding technique. But also, it's a contemplative meditation on the nature of Earth forces in our life.

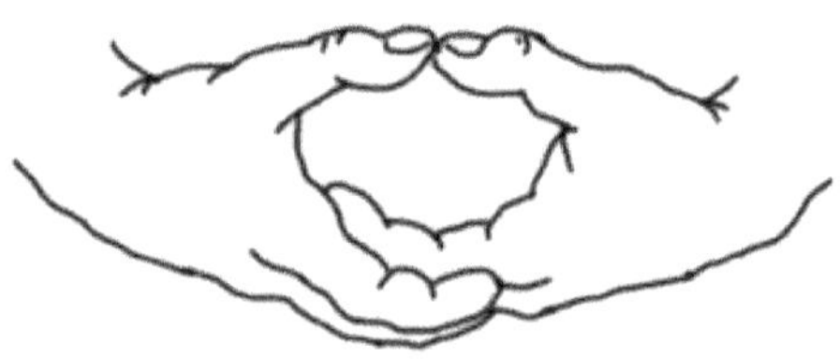

Mudra of Balance

The technique looks like this: in a preferable, comfortable position, relax and close your eyes, putting your hands into balance mudra, like on the illustration above. Focus on your Hara and remain in this focus for next couple of minutes. When you feel it's time to move on, direct your focus onto the center of the Earth – focus on the tiny point in the very center of the core of our planet. Feel the force that you're facing. Feel the power of the planet, its size, density and weight. Keep your focus on the center of the planet and remain in this state of the next 5-20 minutes. At some point, you may literally feel the energy of Earth Ki. When you feel it's time to move on, bring your focus back to your Hara, and after a few more minutes of such focus, open your eyes and finish.

This technique can be practiced in seiza, in lotus sit, or while sitting in an armchair, too.

Sensing Heaven Ki

Heaven energy is light and clear. This energy, for the purpose of meditation and visualization, we associate with our head, that is one of the dantiens (and Diamonds). During practice with this energy, and the head's energy center, we develop our sense of „here and now". We calm down our mind, and we may even experience visions, or our spiritual connection with the world around us.

In a comfortable position of your choice, relax and close your eyes, placing your hands in the mudra of balance. Visualize a bright ball of light energy above your head, a ball that draws its power from Heaven Ki. Breathe in and visualize as the light ball flows down into your head, then into your heart and then into your Hara. Breathe out and visualize as the ball goes back up, from Hara into your heart, then into your head and finally it's back above your head. Repeat this exercise 10 times and notice your sensations and feelings.

Notice your feelings during the practice and after it.

Sensing Heart Ki

Heart Ki, and also the Heart Diamond, is a point of balance between two main cosmic forces – In and Yo, that is earth and heaven Ki. In heart harmony between these two forces is born. When we integrate and develop these energies in our heart, we begin to radiate with spiritual force onto our surrounding environment. In this spiritual light, we heal fears, pain, stress, anger and other unpleasant things. They are replaced with compassion, love and wisdom.

We reach this state through spiritual practice, that is the essence of Reiki. This process, of course, may take many years – it's the process of polishing the Diamond of the Heart.

You may feel this spiritual force through the following exercise. In a relaxed state, while standing, „hug" the air in front of you, on the level of your heart, like you hug a tree. Then reach down, for the energy of Earth, and draw it into your heart. Next, hug the air in front of you and reach for the energy of Heaven, draw it into your heart. Repeat this process 10 times and notice your feelings.

Preliminary Practice – An Introduction to All Techniques

Frans Stiene suggests the following practice that should be learned and then should be performed before any other Reiki technique. It's like an introduction to everything we're going to do, whether it's self-treatment, Gassho meditation or working with another person. Thus, before each practice:

1. **Prepare yourself** – stand or sit comfortable. Relax your muscles, focus your eyes on the floor or ground in front of you, a meter apart. Don't strain your eyes, let them gaze freely. Relax.

2. **Focus on the Hara** – let your mind focus on your abdomen and remain in this state for a few seconds, or a few minutes.

3. **Perform Kenyoku Ho** – it's a technique of spiritual cleansing that also relaxes your breathing.

4. **Again, focus on the Hara, and place your hands in Gassho** – now you can speak, whisper or think the intention of the following practice, or state the goal that

you wish to achieve through this practice.

After you're done, you can go ahead with the main practice. For example, you can start the treatment, or perform meditation or chanting etc. This preliminary practice should precede every other spiritual practice of Reiki. It relaxes the body, mind and breath, and it focus the mind on "here and now".

While the points 1, 2 and 4 are clear, the Kenyoku Ho must be explained.

Kenyoku Ho

Kenyoku Ho is a technique of spiritual cleansing (sometimes known as Reiki "dry bath"). It is a form of misogi. Misogi is a Shinto term, meaning a spiritual cleansing through water – for example, under a waterfall. On Mount Kurama, there are a few places where you can perform misogi cleansing, for example. Traditionally, misogi is practiced by cleansing the hands and mouth with water, before entering a temple or other sacred place. Of course, we're still talking about spiritual cleansing.

Let's take a closer look upon misogi practice. Traditionally, misogi rituals were meant to clear any spiritual impurities by taking a bath or washing the body with water. Those who visit Japan often encounter the rituals of cleansing the hands and mouth before entering a Temple, as mentioned earlier. It's also a form of misogi.[96] According to Shinto teachings, the essence of human being is pure in its nature, but in the process of life, each day, physical and emotional impurities may get sticked to a person's body and soul. The role of cleansing rituals is to cleanse these impurities, before proceeding with spiritual practice in a state of clear, pure inner nature.

---

96 Tubielewicz, J., *Mitologia Japonii*, p. 37.

As you can see, the practice of cleansing is practiced before entering a sacred place, and before beginning a sacred practice. And while Kenyoku Ho is somehow related to traditional misogi of Shinto tradition, in reality the association is not direct, and Kenyoku Ho can be practiced before any spiritual practice. Performing the Kenyoku Ho before Reiki is also meant to prepare the body and the mind, creating a right psychological and physical state of being.

Kenyoku Ho has an energetic aspect and a symbolic aspect to it. It simulates physical washing of impurities. On the energy level, the physical movement and correct breathing stimulates the flow of energy in your arms, hands and inner organs, which leads to energetic cleansing, too. Furthermore, such stimulation increases the ability to channel energies through our hands, and thus, the practice of Kenyoku Ho becomes useful for developing our ability to channel Reiki, as well. Finally, cleansing the energies of your inner organs results in improving your health. On the symbolic level, Kenyoku Ho helps us feel better by "washing" the emotional dirt that was collected on our psyche.

This technique can be used when sitting or standing. It can be performed by itself, or as a part of more complex practice.

1. Relax, either when standing or sitting in seiza.
2. Place your right hand on left shoulder, and then "grab" and bring down any energetic dust from your left shoulder down to your right hip. Repeat this move on the other side of the body. Bring down the energy with left hand from right shoulder to left hip. Repeat this process again, both for left and right side of the body.
3. Then, with your right hand bring down the energy from left arm and hand, from your shoulder down to the tips of

your fingers. Repeat this on your other hand. Then repeat both moves again.

To finish, place your hands in Gassho mudra.

Gassho Kokyu Ho

According to some schools of Yoga, hands put together (like in Gassho) before a given chakra, open this particular energy center. Of course, in case of Reiki we do not work with chakras, but with dantiens. Still, when we talk about terminology only, it's true that Gassho mudra helps to „open" the Heart, one of the Three Diamonds, associated with higher emotions and feelings: compassion, wisdom and love. An extension of this mudra is Gassho meditation.

This meditation should be practiced in seiza, or in lotus sit. But most important, your diaphragm should be able to work without problems, that means your back should be quite straight. The same rule goes for Joshin Kokyu Ho meditation. In Gassho meditation, you breathe in with your nose, and you breathe out with your mouth, allowing for the process of breathing to be calm, yet natural. Breathe with your diaphragm. And that's how the meditation becomes a breathing techniques.

As you breathe and meditate, you may experience different thoughts. „Working" with them, or should I say, a proper way to ignore them, is the essence of Gassho.

As you sit in meditation, breathing, thoughts may come to your mind – it's normal. You may experience many thoughts, or few thoughts, it's an individual matter. A mistake made by meditation rookies is to forcefully pushing these thoughts away. But thoughts are like a cat. A cat wish to visit a place where he is normally unwelcome. When you try to scare the cat away, force him away, he will keep coming back. But leave the cat to his own matters, allow him to see that place you're protecting, and he will come, look around, smell a thing or two, and then – he will leave on his own. This is the nature of things, this is the Tao, and this is what cats are like.

The same goes for thoughts. When you chase them, force them away, push them back, get angry at them, they will come back to you. They will strike back. Thus, in meditation you cannot push your thoughts away. You need to accept them, and let them flow. It looks like this: when a thought comes to your mind, you just notice it, you acknowledge its existence. You may literally say in your mind „oh, a thought..." and then you just go back to breathing. Allow for the thought to be born, allow it to flow through your mind, and disappear. Then, another thought may appear. Treat it just like the previous one. And so on, so on.

After a few weeks, then months of practice, you will experience less and less thoughts, and after years of practice, these unwanted chaotic thoughts disappear completely. Then, you will be able to say that your meditation practiced brought results. The right state of mind means not a complete emptiness, but the acceptance of the nature of your mind.

The meditation itself looks like this:

1. Begin with preliminary practice.
2. Sit down in seiza, with our feet's thumbs placed one on another. You may wish to sit on some yoga mat or similar, or treat yourself with meditation pillow (called zafu).
3. Place your hands in Gassho, and begin to breathe, as described above. As you do this, you may wish to focus your attention on the tips of your hand's middle fingers.
4. Practice this meditation for 10-30 minutes, remembering

about the way of dealing with incoming thoughts, as described earlier.

That's it – this is what Gassho meditation is about.

Joshin Kokyu Ho

The final meditation technique for the Shoden level is the Hara breath techniques. The goal of this practice is to develop the Hara region, an energetic center in your abdomen, by utilizing breath and energy flow controlled by this breath. This meditation also strengthens our connection with Earth Ki through our work with the Hara.

Like all other techniques of healing (and Joshin Kokyu Ho is such technique), practicing this meditation may result in physical, emotional and spiritual reactions, such as another healing crisis, initiation experience, or pulling things out from our unconscious. Remember that such reactions are here to help you heal yourself and realize your Buddha's nature.

Like in other techniques of meditations, Joshin Kokyu Ho, too, has many levels of depth of practice. At first, our practice is very shallow, not very effective. But as time passes, and we make progress with our practice, meditation becomes deeper and deeper, which gives us positive results, such as more peaceful life and mind.

The technique goes as follow:

1. Begin with preliminary practice.
2. Open yourself for the flow of Reiki, and put your hands to Gassho.
3. Then, place your hands on your knees, with inner side of palms facing up.

4. Breathe in with your nose. Because energy follows thoughts and breath, allow yourself (through intentions and thoughts) to draw Reiki through your nose down into the Hara. Just intend for Reiki to flow, and keep your focus on the Hara.

5. On your breathe out, allow the energy to expand from the Hara onto entire body, and then onto the surrounding area, like an expanding balloon.

Repeat the steps 4-5 for 10 to 30 minutes. When you feel dizzy, end your practice. Such dizziness may be caused either by too much energy flowing through your body, or because of too much carbon dioxide flowing in your blood. That last thing is caused by forceful breath, that means – breathing in an unnatural, too controlled way. Remember that you should breathe naturally in any form of meditation.

Each each, you may increase the length of practice by a few seconds, or a minute per day, until you reach 20 minutes of daily practice. To finish the meditation, put your hands back to Gassho.

Joshin Kokyu Ho should be practiced daily for 6 to 12 months, give or take. If you do not practice daily, then you should spend a few years doing this particular meditation. This practice is an introduction to more advanced technique of Seishin Toitsu.

***

To practice Reiki effectively, all you need to do is to work with self-treatments and contemplate upon Five Precepts. But if you wish to deepen your understanding of Reiki's spiritual aspects, as Shoden practitioner you will have a lot more work.

The practice starts, of course, with attunement, after which we begin our individual process of initiation for the particular degree. On the very next day after your Reiki class, you begin your practice. It should be started with self-treatment, which should be practiced daily. Contemplation upon Five Precepts should follow – you should recite these precepts daily. Recitation helps us remember these precepts, while contemplation helps us to free ourselves, step by step, from unwanted thoughts or behaviors. Such contemplation practice can be performed a few times a week.

As a matter of fact, self-treatments and Five Precepts will be a part of your daily life for the rest of your life – or at least for as long as you wish to work with Reiki.

Each self-treatment and contemplation should be preceded with preliminary practice. That's how Kenyoku Ho technique joins your life. This technique can be used as stand-alone, for example every time when we come back home – this way, we're able to cleanse ourselves from unwanted energies or emotions and speed up the flow of our inner Ki.

If you wish, for the first couple of months, you may practice the Ki sensitivity techniques, described earlier. **Warning:** if it happens that you do not feel well after sensitivity practice, try to separate the three exercises: work with Earth Ki on Monday, Heaven Ki on Wednesday, and Heart Ki on Friday, for example. For some people, mixing these techniques may cause an energetic shock.

Kenyoku Ho and the whole preliminary practice should precede all other practices, actually. When you decide to study Reiki deeper in its spiritual aspects, you should support self-treatments and Gokai contemplation with some forms of meditation. First, you can practice Gassho Kokyu Ho for the first three months at least. This meditation helps us calm down and relax our mind, clearing it from unwanted chaotic thoughts. This peaceful mind will be useful on the second level of Reiki. And the technique itself may be useful whenever you happen to experience chaotic thoughts that must be calm down.

Thus, for the first three months, focus on Gokai, Gassho meditation and self-treatments supported by Kenyoku Ho. After three months, you can expand your Gassho practice into Joshin Kokyu Ho, which is an energy meditation developing our Earth Ki energies and connections, and the whole Hara region along with everything that is associated with the Hara. Such practice should be performed for the next three months. After six months in total, you may begin to think about attending Okuden class. Personally, though, I recommend spending at least one year practicing Shoden level, before you move to Okuden.

With all these practices, you may spend an hour and a half, or even two hours practicing Reiki each day.

Beware: if it happens that you experience too many things in your life, like thoughts, emotions, events, a chaos appears and you lose yourself in your thoughts, things to heal etc, then just slow down. Remember about the need for grounding through normal, daily life; then, limit your practice to shorter self-treatments and Gassho meditation that just brings peace to your mind. And if it happens that you have way too many things to work out and heal, just stop your practice entirely, take a break, for a few days, weeks or even months, and fix things.

Daily Grounding

Earlier, I mentioned the need for grounding. Imagine Buddhist monks in a monastery. For some part of their time, they meditate. And for the rest of the time, they work. They have their daily life: the fix the roof, clear the floor, attend the garden, cook and so on. On the path of spiritual growth, no matter what path it is, doing spiritual practice only may lead to mental illness. This happens when spiritual practice is not balanced by daily life.

Spiritual practice is meant for creating good life. Thus, you can't just practice spiritual stuff, you also need to live. You need to work, clean, cook, wash the dishes, write a report for your boss, go with your buddies for coffee, go for a walk. You can't give this up. Daily, ordinary life helps us keep the balance between that which is physical and that which is spiritual. When this balance is kept, your spiritual growth is safe.

It's worth to find inner peace in your daily life, because this is one of the goals of spiritual practice. So that we can learn to feel happy about the daily reality, instead of chasing some mythical idea of happiness, that „will happen when something else will happen because something else will occur".

More than that, sometimes it's worth to practice the technique of sensing the Earth Ki, that was described earlier. As I said, it's also a technique of grounding. When you feel, thanks to your intuition, that too much stuff is going on in your life, spend some time with this grounding technique.

Second Degree: Okuden

The word „Okuden" means „inner teachings". It means teachings focused on your inner self. These are also the teachings dealing with Heaven Ki. Frans Stiene said that second degree practices are meant to help us discover that which is hidden within us. It's about unwanted thoughts or emotions and their sources, but also about our dreams, talents or inborn abilities, which may manifest themselves in our life.

The second Reiki degree is focused mainly on our work with symbols and their names. While each of these symbols can be used in daily treatments, or in very down-to-earth techniques focused on quick results, each of the symbols carries an effect upon one of

Three Diamonds, as well. Many people who complete their Okuden class wonders what do they need the symbols for, actually? Sometimes, it may happen that Reiki class may try to tell the student that second degree is limited to distant healing and „increased flow of energy".

But in reality, the essence of the second degree is its set of symbols and work with the symbols, that gives results on physical, emotional and spiritual levels. As you should known from previous chapters, the symbols affect the harmony of Ki energies within us, and they shape our states of mind. Through their power, working with the symbols leads us forward on our path of self-healing and inner growth.

Except the symbols, Okuden introduces new breathing techniques, which focus on your work with Hara again.

You should know that „entering" the second level of Reiki doesn't mean you can give up the practices of Shoden. To make things simpler, just remember that Okuden adds new things to your practice, it doesn't take anything away. New practices and concepts are added. You still work with self-treatments, with Gokai and different meditations. Gassho meditation and Joshin Kokyu Ho should be continued on the Okuden for another year, at least. Later on, Joshin Kokyu Ho can be replaced with Seishin Toitsu. But to do so, you need to master the first two techniques of meditation.

So when you're on Okuden level, you still work with daily self-treatments and Gokai contemplation. You also practice Kenyoku Ho each day. What is very important is to remember – before you begin your work with the symbols, you need to spend a lot of time working with basic meditations of Gassho and Joshin Kokyu Ho. These meditations develop our foundation needed for safe practice. When you feel like you worked out the meditations properly, you can continue working with them, but now with additional symbols added to your daily practice.

Of course, a Western person is not a Buddhist monk. We don't have that much time each day, so you may wish to create a schedule from now on. Practice self-treatment daily, but meditations and working with the symbols can be practiced on separate days. One day you meditate, the other day you work with the symbols, the other day you work with the Gokai etc.

You still need to take care of your grounding – this cannot be forgotten no matter what level you're on. You need to remember the need for grounding especially when you feel very spiritual – such feelings of being very spiritual, blessed and ignoring the real, physical reality, are rarely a mystical experience. More often, they are a sign you're losing your grounding and beginning to fall into a trap of mental illness. Ground, ground, ground yourself.

First Words on Reiki Symbols

Let's recall a thing or two about the symbols. First, the symbols should be draw with the center of your palm. You can draw them with a finger or two, but drawing them with the middle of your hand is the best way to „establish" the connection with the symbol. You can visualize a symbolic pencil in the middle of your hand that draws the symbol in the air in front of you. The Jumon, the symbol's name, should be spoken out loud three times to active the symbol. It should be remembered that symbol's jumon is mainly a vocal tool – it's our voice that gives „power" to the symbol. According to the tradition of esoteric Buddhism, jumon gives effect due to its sound, that's why reciting the jumon three times should take place out loud. It should be mentioned that the number „three" is not unique for for the system of Reiki, but is a popular „sacred" number in Japan.

The above is a traditional approach. But, if our situation

demands it, we can bend the guidelines a bit. For example, when we're in a place where it's not appropriate to speak the jumons out loud, we can whisper them, or even recite them in our mind.

The strength of the symbol and its effects develop over time, as we progress with our own practice. Some teachers call it a normal process of establishing the symbol. My teacher, Arkadiusz Lisiecki, said to me that the symbols works better and better as we progress with the development of our awareness and spiritual strength; the more our mind is cleared and healed, the stronger the symbols become. In a way, the more we work with Ki energy, the more we heal. And the more we heal, the greater the possibilities of the symbols become. Many practitioners confirm this – the level of spiritual growth has a direct influence over the capabilities of the symbols. Some things that were impossible to do with the symbols in the first couple of months of Okuden practice, may become very, very simple years later.

Hara, once again, is important in our work with the symbols. It's the Hara, from which the breath should originate during chanting; from Hara the sound and the power of the symbol originates, as well. We develop the strength of the symbol by focusing on our Hara when working with the symbols.

You should know that each symbol work independently from each other. In order to activate a given symbol, you just activate it, and you do not have to activate any other symbol before or after the first symbol.

In our work with the symbols, we should notice a common element, no matter what kind of practice we prefer. So: the work with the any of Reiki symbols starts with us learning the theoretical aspects of the symbol. Next, during our practice, we begin to realize things associated with the intentions of the given symbol. It's theory no longer, but also our awareness of things that are present in our life, as represented by the symbols. Next, we begin to try do something about these things. And after some time of spiritual practice, our „trying" comes to an end, and we actually integrate the essence of the symbol into our life. We stop trying to do something with the symbol, and we start to just „be" the symbol. This process may take many years.

All of this actually comes down to one thing – practice. And you should start your practice with the symbols on the very next day after your Okuden class. We have many ways to work with the symbols, some of which I will explain now.

Sensing and Drawing the Symbols

The first thing to start with would be to learn how to sense the symbols. Note that you don't have to be able to sense these symbols to work with them, it's just an interesting exercise to begin with. Each of the symbols can be draw in front of you, as in hanged in the air in front of you. Draw it, then activate it by saying its jumon three times. Then, make a step forward, into the space, in which the symbol has been draw. Close your eyes and try to sense the energy of the symbol, filling the air and space around you. Or, you can simply draw the symbol in front of you, close your eyes, and try to sense its energy, radiating from the space in front of you. This exercise is simple and interesting to try, because by trying to sense the symbol's energy, we're developing our innate understanding of a given symbol.

During the first three weeks after your Okuden class, you should work with each of the first three symbols one after another. Spend the first week on drawing and activating the first symbol multiple times. Spend the second week on working with the second symbol, and the third week on the third symbol. Such intense yet simple practice will help you get used to drawing the symbol and to its energy. It's a very down-to-earth approach for the first three weeks. After that, you can begin the actual spiritual practice.

Meditating with the Symbol

You can meditate with each Reiki symbol, remembering, though, about the order of the symbols. The symbol meditation is quite simple. By now you should be familiar with the Gassho meditation. Thus, start Gassho meditation now, remembering about the preliminary practice first. Calm down your mind. Next draw the symbol in front of you and activate it by saying its name three times.

Now you can either close your eyes or keep them open, in both cases keeping your focus on the visualized symbol in front of you, using your „inner eye". Each couple of minutes, you can repeat the symbol's jumon, but your sole focus on the symbol's shape will be enough in case of this meditation. If you're visualization skills are not good enough, you can paint the symbol or print it and place it in front of you. Then just focus on the actual physical symbol for the purpose of this meditation. In this meditation, the Reiki symbol is just a point of focus – but in many traditions of esoteric Buddhism of Japan, such practice is very traditional and gives real positive effects.

Such meditation can be continued for 10 to 60 minutes each time.

And the order of symbols? After completing your Okuden class, you should start your practice with the first symbol, CKR. While we can spend three weeks on remembering how to draw the symbols from memory, as mentioned earlier, the actual practice begins with intense practice with the CKR. You should spend at least half a year working with the CKR. During this time, you should not truly work with the other two symbols. After six months, begin another half a year of work with the SHK, and six months later, begin working with the HS for another half a year. This is a proper order of spiritual practice with the symbols.

Chanting the Jumons

Another, a bit more advanced practice of working with the symbols, is the practice of chanting their jumons.

An example of mala. The brighter bead is the stupa, also known as the "guru" bead or "Buddha" bead.

If you own a Buddhist mala[97], you can practice the chanting with this meditation prayer beads. The basic practice of chanting suggest to repeat each jumon 10 thousand times, and connect it with visualizing the symbol. We do this in the following way:

1. Begin the practice. Sit down, perform the preliminary practice, and focus on your Hara next. Define your intention, which is to repeat the jumon 10 thousand times.
2. Open yourself for the flow of Reiki and pick a mala. Draw the symbol in front of you, or just visualize it in your mind.

---

97 Mala is a Buddhist prayer beads. Usually, the mala has 108 beads with 109th bead called "the stupa", or the guru bead, which marks the beginning and end of the mala.

3. Next, start to count the beads. Hold the first bead near the Stupa (guru bead, the main bead), and recite the jumon out loud. You can whisper it, say it aloud, but the best choice is to speak it aloud and vibrate your voice, like you can hear in popular Buddhist chants. Vibrating the jumon and visualizing the symbol should be performed while you focus your mind on your Hara. Work with your diaphragm.
4. Hold the next bead, and repeat the 3rd step.
5. Repeat the jumon at least 108 times – it's a standard number of beads on a mala. When you reach the final bead right before the Stupa, you can end your practice, or continue it for another 108 repetitions. If you continue your practice, do not cross the stupa, but rather turn around and count the beads backward.[98]
6. When you finish your chanting practice, just put the mala away and close the flow of Reiki, thanking for the energy and the practice. Repeat the Kenyoku Ho and focus on your Hara for a minute or two.

Each day you can repeat the jumons a couple thousand times, but even the basic practice of 108, 216 or 324 repetitions per day should be enough. When we chant the symbol, we activate it and allow its energy to affect us.

In the practice explained above, we chant the symbols like this: *cho-ku-rei, cho-ku-rei, cho-ku-rei...* Another way to chant the symbol is to repeat: *cho, cho, cho* (108 times), then *ku, ku, ku* (108 times) and finally *rei, rei, rei* (108). But personally, I suggest to stick to the first way of chanting, which gives a proper number of repetitions and symbol's activations. For example, 108 repetitions

---

98 Not crossing the stupa bead is traditional – to not cross the stupa is a symbol of never ending practice.

gives 36 activations, 216 repetitions gives 72 activations.

Begin your entire chanting practice with 10 thousand repetitions of the CKR symbol. You can practice this along with Joshin Kokyu Ho meditation. The first symbol builds the foundation for the future practice. After a few months, or even half a year, when you're done with 10 thousand repetitions of the CKR, proceed with 10 thousand repetitions of the SHK, and then, after another couple of months, with 10 thousand repetitions of the HS. Later on, this will be continued with 10 thousand repetitions of the DKM, which is the subject of the third degree of Reiki. Nevertheless, it's a basic practice. If you wish, you can repeat this entire practice by another 10 thousand repetitions of the CKR, then 10 thousand repetitions of the SHK and so on.

It's a good idea to mix symbol's meditation and chanting of the symbol. If it happens that you can't chant the symbol at the given day, at least you can meditate with it through meditation. You can chant the symbols on your own, or in a group. The more people chant the symbol, the stronger the energy around us becomes.

Calligraphy and Painting the Symbols

Sometimes it seems that the only influence of Zen Buddhism over Reiki can be found in calligraphy, poetry or etiquette of Reiki.[99] Calligraphy is not just about physically painting a symbol, but also on achieving a state of meditation during this physical activity. The skill of calligraphy was meant to clear the mind, so that our true nature can be seen.[100]

At some point of my own practice, as a result of working with the CKR that is associated with many down-to-earth activities, and thus also with artistic expression, I have noticed that you do not

---

99 Szymańska, B., *Chiński Buddyzm Chan*, .p 182.

100 Ibidem, p. 186.

have to paint the symbols like Japanese master of calligraphy. Let's make things clear: if you have the opportunity to learn real Japanese calligraphy alone with all its meditative aspects, seize this opportunity!

But even if you do not learn the actual spiritual way of calligraphy, Reiki can provide you with a substitute, that – with time and patience – can become a form of meditation. I'm taking about the practice of painting the symbols based on their contour. I never had the opportunity to learn the „real" calligraphy, so I found another practice: I print the weak gray contours of each symbols and use an Indian ink (Chinese ink) to paint the symbols based on these contours.

While I fill the contours with the ink, I let Reiki flow through me, and with time I've noticed that it's enough to enter a meditative state of mind. It's probably not as subtle as calligraphy meditation, but it's a form of meditative and artistic expression – the peace and happiness results of this practice. You may try this as well.

Hatsurei Ho

In the past I believed that this meditation can be practiced by anyone on the second degree of Reiki. But at some point, I decided to move this practice to the third degree due to its strong effects. The choice to practice this meditation now, or wait till Shinpiden, is yours. Generally, if you have spent enough time on practicing Reiki, and you understand Buddhist and Taoist concepts, practicing Hatsurei Ho on Okuden will be appropriate. And if you don't feel strong enough, leave this practice till Shinpiden.

Frans Stiene believes that Hatsurei Ho is a modern practice, that evolved from more traditional Seishin Toitsu. Hatsurei Ho merges together Kenyoku Ho, Joshin Kokyu Ho and Seishin Toitsu. Traditionally, the Reiki practitioner was beginning his journey with preliminary practice including Kenyoku Ho, and he used to practice Joshin Kokyu Ho for six to twelve months. Then, the practitioner could move to Seishin Toitsu.

These days, all these things seem to be merged together and the Hatsurei Ho was born.

Below you can see an outline of the more traditional Hatsurei Ho practice. It's interesting that modern practice is focused on energy work, while older versions of Hatsurei Ho are focused on mind work. This more traditional version begins with clearing the mind, and then focusing on some idea or a thought. In case of Reiki, these ideas and concepts are Waka poems of Meiji emperor.

1. Sit down comfortably and gaze at the floor in front of you. Breathe naturally.
2. Put your hands in Gassho and focus your attention on your hands. It will make the Heart Ki flow between the heart and the hands. Relax.
3. Focus on the Waka poem, or some other spiritual idea. In case of Waka poem, the goal is to contemplate its spiritual nature and understand it fully.

That's it – just contemplate upon the Waka poem. Such contemplation should be practiced anywhere between 30 to 60 minutes. A modern Reiki teacher, Mochizuki Toshitaka, noticed that modern practitioners do not have to contemplate upon Waka poems themselves, but they can find a different way to focus the mind – like focusing on Buddhist sutra, or a modern poem or quote, that moves heart and mind of the practitioner. [101]

***

---

101 Stiene, B., Stiene F., *Japanese Art of Reiki*, p. 90.

Now you know the techniques that can be used for working with the symbols. To work successfully with the Okuden, you may begin by meditating with the symbols – this meditation will focus on learning how to draw the symbols, and how to say their jumons, in addition it will teach you how to feel the energies of the symbols. Next, you can proceed to a preferred main practice – whether it's main meditation, or chanting, or the practice of both techniques at the same time. You may also wish to begin calligraphy meditating if you only feel it's right for you.

Of course, throughout all the Okuden degree, you still practice self-treatments, contemplation with the Five Precepts and meditations learned on Shoden.

I should point you out to one more thing related to working with the symbols. They shape the mood of the present moment and place. In other words, when you, for example, practice with the CKR, your life may seem more grounded and down-to-earth. Our focus may be directed mainly to things that are material, physical, like diet, hobby, work, money. It's normal, because this is the range of this symbol's „intentions". And while working with the SHK, you may experience greater interest in our inner self and that which is related to energies of Heaven. And things like interest in spiritual or intuitive insights into the nature of things may become part of your life as you practice with the HS. Finally, a sense of integrity may be part of your DKM practice.

You are free to repeat your work with the symbols. Or, you should really repeat it – I consider first two years of Okuden practice to be merely a preliminary practice. Two years are not enough to achieve everything that is to be achieved on spiritual path, or even due to working with the symbols. Thus, after completing your path of three (or four) symbols, you should turn around and repeat this path all over again, and all over again once more. You will notice that many things that never occurred to you during your first approach to symbols will actually occur after many years of practice, when the symbols open some new doors in your life. This process goes for each of the symbols. By going back to previous practices with your new experience and strength, you are able to heal many new things that you were unaware previously.

Of course, the order of practice is important. When you are decided to go back and start the practice all over again, but this time, from a „stronger" and more experienced start point, you still need to begin with basic practices and make your way to more advanced practices. This is a guarantee of safe and successful spiritual practice.

Third Degree: Shinpiden

The third degree is often presented as the final step of Reiki journey, when all that we can experience is the final enlightenment (more like lighting a light bulb, than the soul). On the other hand, some people present Shinpiden as a path of many obstacles, difficulties and traps, that require the practitioner to be very patient, humble and careful, because the path of spiritual growth is not an easy one. The truth, like in Buddhism, lies in between.

Shinpiden is the moment of our journey when the flow of Reiki becomes very strong. The term „Shinpiden" translates as secret teachings. It's about discovering the secrets that lie within us.

It's a degree focused on further self-healing of the practitioner, a moment, when we experience both the pain and the blessing of spirituality. We should not associate the third degree with becoming a Reiki teacher. In traditional Reiki, Shinpiden level was never the same thing as the teacher level. When the practitioner of

Shinpiden was ready, he was becoming the assistant of the teacher, and after some time of being an assistant, we was promoted for a teacher himself.

In traditional Reiki in the time of Usui, Reiki was divided into many degrees. The lowest one, sixth degree was called Shoden. It was divided into four sub-degrees: Loku-To (6th), Go-To (5th), Yon-To (4th) and San-To (3rd). To move from level to level, the student had to meet with the teacher a few times a month, learn and practice, before the teacher allowed the student to progress onto the next level. During such meetings, the student recited the Five Precepts, recite the Waka poems, practiced the Joshin Kokyu Ho, and received the Reiju. The next degree was Okuden, and it was divided into Okuden-Zenki and Okuden-Koko, when the student learned the symbols. Finally, there was Shinpiden, it was the first degree. The person could receive the title of Shinan-Kaku, an assistant to the actual teacher of Reiki. When the student was ready, he could become a full Shinan, the teacher.[102] As you should be aware, these days, it's a bit different.

And thus, it's worth to make the distinction between the level of Shinpiden and actually being a Reiki teacher. Many people believe that Reiki teacher is a person who completed his or hers Reiki journey. On the contrary, I cannot see a new Buddha among Reiki teachers. No, Reiki teachers, in reality, are normal, ordinary practitioners of Reiki, just like those of Shoden or Okuden. The difference being only in the scale of practice and number of tools (another symbol, another meditation).

You should perceive the matter like this: the Reiki teacher is merely a Reiki Shinpiden practitioner who becomes the teacher for the time of class and workshop only, to pass the knowledge and support the students. But when he runs no class nor workshop, he

---

102 Usarzewicz W., *Droga Reiki*, p. 60.

or she is just a Shinpiden person who still face the need of self-healing and self-growth.

The third level of Reiki once again is based on practices such as self-treatments, contemplation of Gokai or Gassho meditation. At the same time, by the time you reach Shinpiden, about three years should have passed after attending the Shoden class. If you have been practicing Shoden and Okuden on regular basis, by now it's a good time to shift from Joshin Kokyu Ho to Seishin Toitsu, and the chanting of first three symbols should be changed to intense work with the fourth symbol. It may appear that on Shinpiden there is less work than on the first two degrees, but it's merely an illusion. In reality, while the number of techniques and meditations is smaller, their strength and intensity is greater, increasing the „difficulty level" of your practice.

Practices for the Fourth Symbol of DKM

Another level of Reiki means another symbol – the last of Reiki symbols. Basically, each and every technique used to work with the symbols of Okuden, such as chanting or visualization, can be applied to the fourth symbol, so there's no need to repeat the instructions here. Just go back to the Okuden techniques for working with the symbols, and replace these symbols with the fourth one - DKM.

Thus, you can meditate with the DKM by visualizing it, or focusing on symbols' painting. You can paint it yourself through calligraphy meditation. And you can chant this symbol, as well.

Seishin Toitsu

By the time you reach Shinpiden level, you should have two years of Joshin Kokyu Ho practice behind you. Now you can replace it with another meditation of Seishin Toitsu. The quality and effectiveness of this meditation depends on how much time and effort you put into Joshin Kokyu Ho. Seishin Toitsu is an advanced practice and it can lead to serious healing of both mind and body, so you should not jump to it until you've spend a couple of years working with previous Reiki techniques, including the symbols.

In addition, if you practice both Seishin Toitsu and you work with the DKM at the same time, you should actually limit the time you spend on these practices, and make them less intense, especially for the first couple of months, because the effects of these two practices are very strong.

Seishin Toitsu is a meditation that, once again, can result in greater sensitivity to energies in our hands, and it may develop our connection with the Earth Ki.

1. Begin with the preliminary practice.
2. With hands in Gassho, focus on your Hara.
3. Breathe in, and feel as Reiki flows from your Hands, through your arms, down the torso and down into your Hara.
4. On the breathe out, feel as the energy flows backward, up the torso, through your arms back to your hands.
5. Practice this meditation for 5 to 60 minutes. Begin with shorter meditation, and as months pass by, increase the time.

If you're not able to feel the actual flow of energy, don't worry. Remember that the energy follows thoughts. Thus, you can just focus on your hands, and the switch the focus to your Hara. Then again, focus on your hands and again on your Hara. The energy will flow between these two points of focus.

***

The DKM is a key to enlightenment. It opens the gates to practices, practices that lead to the state of enlightenment. But the fourth symbol is also a very powerful meditation symbol originating from the traditions of esoteric Buddhism. Its subtle power transcends everything that you worked with on previous degrees of Reiki. That's why it must be said – you should not overdo your work with the DKM. Your practice with the DKM should be less intensive than your work with the previous symbols. Your daily practice should focus, once again, on self-treatments, Gokai, Gassho meditation, and Joshin Kokyu Ho, later replaced by Seishin Toitsu.

The actual work with the DKM symbol – meditations, visualizations, chanting – can be practiced no more than once a week for the first couple of months. Then, you can increase the amount of time spend on the DKM to twice or thrice a week. Here you should remember about the following safety rule: if too many things start to happen in your life, like too many fears, emotions and memories come out from your unconscious, and you're not able to deal with them, you need to stop your work with the DKM, calm down, heal and fix things. Only when your life becomes quiet and peaceful again, you can go back to gentle DKM practice. And so on, so on – never take more than you can carry in case of things to heal.

Our task on the path of Shinpiden is to recognize our Shadows and heal them.

Third Degree – Integration of Personality

In Buddhism, there is a concept of Anatman, that says „self", as

„me", does not exists. „Me/Self" is merely an illusion. Sangharakszita describes is nicely in his book „What is Dharma?" He explains that the concept of Anatman says that „self" is an illusion because for one, it is dynamic, and second, each person is „made" of different „selfs". The dynamics and constant change of the „self" is what makes us trust in our ability to change ourselves, for better or worse. We need to take full responsibility for this change. While this is quite positive to know, the second thing, the diversity of „selfs" in our psyche, often cause troubles in our life.

Sangharakszita says that sometimes, one „self" has a voice in the evening, and another „self" gets its voice in the morning, which do not agree with the first self. It's not schizophrenia, but a normal aspect of human psyche, recognized by modern psychology. Here we talk about our many faces, parts of our general character, personality. While we're talking about many faces of our personality, we're not talking about masks that we put on, one for our lover, one for our family, one for our boss. No, we're talking about something closer to Buddhist aspect of the Anatman. We're talking about our different dreams, wishes, and thoughts, that sometimes get our attention, and on other time, they remain silent.

As such, one „self" may wish to go vegan, while another „self" will still ask for meat. One „self" may wish to practice meditation, and another „self" may wish to play computer games. One „self" may prefer to be alone, another „self" seeks other people. And each of these „selfs" will dominate at some time, and go silent at another time. Our goal is to seek harmony between different „selfs" so that each of our „selfs" is contented. The great amount of these „selfs" is a result of many causes, most of which we find in our subconscious. These selfs are results of our rising, life experiences and dreams we wish to achieve, or our expectation from the world or ourselves, our goals and behaviors. Out of all of this, different „selfs" are born – each of them a part of our personality.

Here's a simple, down-to-earth example – one self may wish to be rich, while another self screams in panic that rich people are evil and this second self do not wish to become evil. An inner conflict is born as result. Many young people often recognize this when they experience the inner conflict – part of us may wish one thing, the other part of us may wish to deny it. Our inner life is full of such contradictions. In order to achieve enlightenment in a Buddhist sense of this word, we need to integrate different „selfs" into one, so that we can become free of them later.

I mention all of this because the final level of Reiki, Shinpiden, is the process of integration of the previous two degrees. On Shinpiden, you may become aware of the number of different „selfs" you carry within you. Today you may wish for one thing to happen, tomorrow you may wish for another thing to happen. Today something will seem to be normal, tomorrow it may seem to be unethical. Today you may wish to live in the city, tomorrow you may dream for a cabin in the mountains. While the first and second degree of Reiki helped you to become aware of different thoughts, emotions, goals, behaviors, habits etc, and you've learned to let go of them, the Shinpiden can show you different sides of your personality, sides presented as different, complex parts of the same thing – you. Your task is to recognize these different selfs, learn them, understand them, recognize their sources, heal them and integrate them together into one whole that is steady and united.

The process of healing and integration may take many years. If this integration won't take place, then the peace of mind and state of Unity, as described in this book, may never come.

***

We've reached the end of explaining the practices of the three degrees.

Summary

Mikao Usui created a wonderful method of spiritual healing. All you have to do is to complete your Shoden class, and then, do self-treatments, and Reiki will affect your life in a positive manner, introducing harmony and unity into your life, promoting inner peace and healthy lifestyle, even in our chaotic, „Western" life. At the same time, this wonderful yet simple practice of Reiki has a second, deeper aspect to itself. By studying it and applying it into your life, you may experience not only happiness and peace, like the basic practice does, but also a deeper, spiritual understanding of our true nature, which can lead each person to enlightenment.

Yet it must be remembered that the sources of Reiki, the roots of this practice, that reach as far as to Buddhist or Shinto, are merely here to help you understand the practice. They do not make the essence of Reiki. The essence of Reiki is the practice – shaping the clear and peaceful mind, and channeling the energy to yourself and others, which is beneficial to all living beings.

I hope that this book helped you understand that Five Principles, Gassho mudra, or breathing techniques are not merely an add-on to Reiki treatments, but are, in reality, an integral element of the entire practice.

I wish you to benefit from the content of this book, yet, at the same time, I ask you: benefit from additional knowledge, but never try to put knowledge above the practice itself, because your individual practice is the essence of Reiki – with it, you can discover the individual and personal spiritual truths that dwell within your own soul and lead you to your own, personal and individual self-healing.

Appendixes

Glossary of Japanese Terms

Because in Reiki we deal with a couple of Japanese terms, here is a list of such terms translated, as associated with the practice of Usui Shiki Ryoho Reiki.

Bokusen – divination.

Chiryo – treatment, healing.

Chobuku – exorcism.

Den – legend, tradition, teachings.

Denju – passing on the teachings.

Do – method of healing, a way, a path.

Dojo – a physical place where teachings are passed.

Enjudo – a placed of healing, located in a temple or monastery.

Enzui bu – left or right side of the neck.

Gakkai – community, organization.

Gassho – means „to put hands together”.

Gedoku – detox.

Genki – a ghost, a spirit.

Go shimbo – spiritual teaching (Dharma) for the protection of the body, a ritual of Tendai tradition.

Gokai – Five Principles.

Gyo – ascetic practices.

Gyosei – poems wrote down by Meiji Emperor.

Hara – abdomen, the name for the first dantien.

Hatsurei – to create greater amount of spiritual energy.

Hibiki – sound, echo, vibration. The sensation being part of Byosen Reikan Ho practice.

Hiei zan – mount Hiei near Kyoto.

Ho – a method, a technique.

Hikkei – companion, a manual.

Honu no reiko – spiritual light, existing in every living being.

In – Yin.

Ichinyo – Unity.

Joshin – to focus the mind.

Jumon – charm, spell, mantra.

Kami – a common name for deities in Shinto.

Kanji – a Chinese character.

Kenyoku – dry bath.

Ki – life force.

Ki Ko – to cultivate life force (Qigong)

Kiriku – a character, sourced in Hrih syllable, associated with Amida Buddha.

Kito – incantation.

Kokyu – breathing.

Koto bu – the back of the head.

Kotodama – words carrying spirit.

Kurama yama – mount Kurama near Kyoto.

Ling Chi – Chinese spelling of Reiki character.

Misogi – cleansing.

Naga-iki – long breath.

Nentatsu – to send thoughts, or intentions.

Nichirin in – Sun mudra.

Okuden – inner teachings.

Reiju – to offer spiritual energy, to bless.

Ryoho – healing method.

Sansho – trice.

Satori – spiritual awakening.

Seishin – ghost, spirit, soul, mind, intention.

Seiza – correct way of sitting.

Sensei – teacher, master.

Shiki – The Way.

Shihan – teacher, one who teach.

Shinpiden – secret teachings.

Shirushi – symbol

Shoden – first teachings.

Shugenja – Shugendo practitioner, one who learned the power or gained experience.

Teate – healing through touch.

Tenohira – healing through touch, but win standardized way, for example, through hand positions.

Toitsu – to unite, to bring together.

Uchu-rei – universal mind.

Wa – harmony

Waka – a poem made of 31 syllables.

Yamabushi – Shugendo practitioner, one who lives in the mountains.

Yo – Yang.

Zaike – lay monk.

Zento bu – forehead.

Bibliography

Books and articles

1. Baynes, C. F., *The I Ching or Book of Changes. The Richard Wilhelm Translation.* [Przed.] Jung, C. G., Wyd. Routledge & Kegan Paul, London 1951.

2. Chia, M. *Taoistyczna joga ezoteryczna. Budzenie uzdrawiającej energii Tao.* Wyd. ABA, Warszawa 2003.

3. Dale, C., *The Subtle Body. An Encyclopedia of Your Energetic Anatomy.* Wyd. Sounds True, Boulder 2009.

4. De Martino, R., Fromm, E., Suzuki, D. T., *Buddyzm zen i psychoanaliza.* Wyd. Rebis, Poznań 2006.

5. Dotson, B. M., *Reiki and Qigong.* [W:] Reiki News Magazine, Lato 2013, tom 12, nr 2. Wyd. Vision Publications, s. 33-38.

6. Groppi, J. A., *Reiki Can Heal the Shadow Self.* [W:] Reiki News Magazine, Jesień 2011, tom 10, nr 3. Wyd. Vision Publications, s. 37-41.

7. Hansen, C., Toropov, B., *Taoizm dla żółtodziobów, czyli wszystko, co powinieneś wiedzieć o...* [Przeł.] Musielak, S., Wyd. Dom wydawniczy Rebis, Poznań 2003.

8. Hall, J.W., *Japonia od czasów najdawniejszych do dzisiaj.* [Tłum.] Czyżewska-Madajewicz, K., Wyd. Państwowy Instytut Wydawniczy, Warszawa 1979.

9. Hayashi, C., Petter, F.A., Yamaguchi, T., *The Hayashi Reiki Manual. Traditional Japanese Healing Techniques From the Founder of the Western Reiki System.* Wyd. Lotus Press, Twin Lakes 2003.

10. Havlick, M. J., Jr [red.], *The Archetype of Initiation. Sacred Space, Ritual Process, and Personal Transformation. Lectures and Essays by Robert L. Moore.* Wyd. Xlibris Corporation 2001.

11. Hazama, J., *The Characteristics of Japanese Tendai.* [W:] Japanese

Journal of Religious Studies 1987, 14/2-3, s. 101-112.

12. Hoff, B., *Tao Kubusia Puchatka*. Wyd. Rebis, Poznań 1992.

13. Hwa, J. T., *Droga Tai Chi*. Wyd. Ravi, Łódź 1997.

14. Jakimowicz, A., Jakimowicz-Shah, M., *Mitologia indyjska*. Wyd. Artystyczne i filmowe, Warszawa 1982.

15. J. Ś. Dalajlama, *Moc współczucia. Wybór wykładów*. [Przeł.] Grabiak, J., Żarnawski M., Wyd. Dom wydawniczy Rebis, Poznań 2001.

16. J. Ś. Dalajlama, *Przebudzenie umysłu, rozświetlanie serca*. Wyd. Rebis, Poznań 2003.

17. Jwing-Ming, Y., *Korzeń Chińskiego Qigong. Sekrety zdrowia, długowieczności i oświecenia*. Wyd. YMAA, Kraków 2000.

18. Kadayam, S., *The Secret of Many Blessings, 1-5*. [W:] International House of Reiki, dostęp on-line 16.12.2013: <http://www.ihreiki.com/blog/article/the_secret_of_many_blessings_part_1_of_5_the_first_miracles>

19. Kerr, A., *Japonia utracona*. [Tłum.] Kwiecińska-Decker, M., Wyd. Prószyński i S-ka, Warszawa 1999.

20. Kosior, K., *Budda*. Wyd. WAM, Kraków 2007.

21. Kubiak, A.E., *Jednak New Age*. Wyd. Jacek Santorski & Co, Agencja wydawnicza, Warszawa 2005.

22. Kunstler, M., J., *Mitologia chińska*. Wyd. Artystyczne i filmowe, Warszawa 1985.

23. Lubeck, W., Hosak, M., *The Big Book of Reiki Symbols. The Spiritual Tradition of Symbols and Mantras of the Usui System of Natural Healing*. Wyd. Lotus Press, 2009.

24. Lubke, G., von., *Dawna mądrość na nowe czasy. Rozmowy z uzdrawiaczami i szamanami XXI wieku*. Wyd. Czarna Owca, 2009.

25. Ogarek-Czoj, H., *Mitologia Korei*. Wyd. Artystyczne i filmowe, Warszawa 1988.

26. Petter, F.A., *Reiki Fire. New Information about the Origins of the Reiki Power. A Complete Manual*. Wyd. Lotus Press, Twin Lakes 2010.

27. Petter, F.A., Reiki. *The Legacy of Dr. Usui. Rediscovered documents on the origins and developments of the Reiki system, as well as new aspects of the Reiki energy.* Wyd. Lotus Press, Twin Lakes 2010.

28. Petter, F. A., *This is Reiki. Transformation of Body, Mind and Soul. From the Origins to the Practice.* Wyd. Lotus Press, Twin Lakes 2012.

29. Rand, W. L., *Interview With Hiroshi Doi Sensei.* [W:] Reiki News Magazine, Wiosna 2014, tom 13, nr 1. Wyd. Vision Publications.

30. Rand, W. L., *Japanese Reiki Techniques.* [W:] Reiki News Magazine, Lato 2011, tom 10, nr 2. Wyd. Vision Publications, s. 28-33.

31. *Reiki Symbols.* [W:] International House of Reiki, dostęp on-line: <www.ihreiki.com/blog/article/reiki_symbols>

32. Rinpoche, K. T. [autor], Gyamtso, Y. [tłum.], Namgyal, T. [red.], *Medicine Buddha Teachings.* Wyd. Snow Lion Publications, Ithaca 2004.

33. Rinpocze, S., *Tybetańska Księga Życia i Umierania.* Wyd. Mandala, Warszawa 2010.

34. Sangharakszita, *Czym jest Dharma? Podstawy nauki Buddy.* Wyd. Wydawictwo A, Kraków 2005.

35. Sangharakszita, *Czym jest Sangha? Natura duchowej społeczności.* Wyd. Wydawnictwo A, Kraków 2007.

36. Sangharakszita, *Wprowadzenie do Buddyzmu.* Wyd. Wydawnictwo A, Kraków 2002.

37. Skarbek, J., *Reiki i co dalej...?* Wyd. Studio Astropsychologii, Białystok 2001.

38. Stiene, B., Stiene, F., *The Japanese Art of Reiki. A Practical Guide to Self-Healing.* Wyd. O Books, New York 2005.

39. Stiene, B., Stiene, F., *The Reiki Sourcebook.* Wyd. O Books, New York 2008.

40. Stiene, F., *The Secret of Reiju.* [W:] International House of Reiki, dostępn on-line: <http://www.ihreiki.com/blog/article/the_secret_of_reiju>

41. Suzuki, D. T., *Wprowadzenie do Buddyzmu Zen.* [Przed.:] Jung, C. G., [Tłum.:] Grabowski A., Grabowska M., Wyd. Vis-a-vis etiuda, Kraków 2011.

42. Szyjewski, A., *Szamanizm.* Wyd. WAM, Kraków 2005.

43. Szymańska, B., *Chiński Buddyzm Chan.* Wyd. WAM, Kraków 2009.

44. Tubielewicz, J., *Mitologia Japonii.* Wyd. Artystyczne i filmowe, Warszawa 1986.

45. Usarzewicz, W., *Droga Reiki.* Wyd. Ezokultus, Wrocław 2012.

46. Usarzewicz, W., *Inicjacja do Reiki jako proces, nie zaś oświecenie instant.* [W:] Taraka.pl, dostęp on-line: <http://www.taraka.pl/inicjacja_reiki_proces_nie>

47. Williams, P., *Buddyzm Mahajana.* [Tłum.] Smagacz, H., Wyd. A, Kraków 2000.

48. Winn, M., *Alchemia taoizmu.* Wyd. A, 2006.

Other sources

1. Jusan Butsu, The Thirteen Buddhas of the Shingon School. <http://www.shingon.org/deities/jusanbutsu/jusanbutsu.html>

2. *Kalama Sutra.* <http://www.accesstoinsight.org/lib/authors/soma/wheel008.html>

3. Buddhist Deities: <http://www.onmarkproductions.com/html/buddhism.shtml>

About the Author

Nathaniel is a writer, publisher, musician (he plays Native American flutes) and, of course, Reiki practitioner. He wrote multiple books on various subjects such as Reiki, healing, psychic abilities and magick. He lives and works in Poland, EU.

Find him on-line:

- http://www.goodreads.com/author/show/3436123.Nathaniel
- https://twitter.com/astateofmind

explore more NATHANIEL's books
on reiki, healing, and magick

available as ebooks and paperbacks